OVERNIGHT SENSATIONS

Recipes From Virginia's Finest Bed & Breakfasts

Tracy & Phyllis Winters

Winters Publishing
P.O. Box 501
Greensburg, Indiana 47240

(812) 663-4948

© 1992 Tracy M. Winters and Phyllis Y. Winters
All rights reserved
Printed in the United States of America

PHOTO CREDITS:
Front cover: From The Manor at Taylor's Store, Smith Mountain Lake, VA
Back cover: By John Keith, from The Madison House, Lynchburg, VA

The information about the inns and the recipes were supplied by the inns themselves. The rate information was current at the time of submission, but is subject to change. Every effort has been made to assure that the book is accurate. Neither the inns, authors, or publisher assume responsibility for any errors, whether typographical or otherwise.

No part of this book may be reproduced in any form or by any means without the prior written approval of the publisher, except by a reviewer who may quote brief passages.

Library of Congress Card Catalog Number 92-90875
ISBN 0-9625329-2-4

Dedication

To our daughters,
Rebekah Ann
&
Rachel Ann
With Love

Acknowledgements

We would like to thank The Bed & Breakfast Association of Virginia for working with us on this project, and all of the innkeepers who took valuable time to select recipes and fill out questionnaires. Special thanks to Mary Lynn Tucker for her help.
It is because of all of their efforts that we were able to make this book a reality.

Preface

Welcome to the kitchens of Virginia's finest Bed & Breakfasts! The innkeepers featured in this cookbook are pleased to share with you some special recipes that their B&B guests delight in. They also invite you to visit their B&Bs to partake of the whole B&B experience - unique settings, lovely homes, warm hospitality, delicious food, and interesting people.

All B&Bs represented here are members of The Bed and Breakfast Association of Virginia, a non-profit state-wide trade association. All members agree to adhere to the highest standards in hospitality, service, and facilities. These standards are assured by an annual inspection program and monitored by a guest comment card program. It is the goal of the Association to foster quality B&B and Country Inn accommodations for travellers in Virginia.

We hope that you will enjoy this "taste of Virginia" and that you will enjoy the taste of Virginia hospitality offered you as a guest at any of these fine Bed and Breakfasts.

> Mary Lynn Tucker
> President
> Bed and Breakfast
> Association of Virginia

CONTENTS

Muffins	6
French Toast, Pancakes & Waffles	15
Breads	25
Egg, Meat & Cheese Dishes (Soufflés, Quiches & Casseroles)	32
Assorted Baked Goods	48
Miscellaneous Fare	59
Not Just For Breakfast...	67
Desserts	88
Visiting Virginia	104
State Map	106
Index Of Inns	108
Order Form	112

MUFFINS

BLUEBERRY CORN MUFFINS WITH HAM AND ORANGE BUTTER

1 1/2 cups yellow cornmeal
1 cup all-purpose flour
1/3 cup sugar
1 tablespoon baking powder
1 teaspoon salt
1 cup rinsed, drained fresh blueberries

1/2 cup chopped, fresh sweet corn (or frozen or canned)
1 cup milk
1/2 cup cream
1/2 cup butter, melted
2 eggs, beaten slightly
36 thin slices smoked ham (3/4 to 1 lb.)

Orange Butter:
6 tablespoons butter, softened

Grated peel of 2 small or 1 large orange
2 teaspoons brown sugar

Combine first five ingredients in large bowl. Remove 1/3 cup and toss lightly with blueberries in a small bowl. Combine corn, milk, cream, melted butter and eggs in a medium bowl. Pour into dry ingredients and stir just until thoroughly combined. Gently fold in blueberries. Divide batter among 18 muffin cups (sprayed with non-stick spray) and bake 15 - 20 minutes at 400°. Cool muffins 3 - 5 minutes in pan before removing. Slice each muffin in half. Mix Orange Butter ingredients. Spread bottom half of muffin with a teaspoon of butter. Add 2 slices ham, replace tops and serve. Can make ahead, wrap in foil, and reheat for 15 minutes in a 350° oven.

Submitted by:

Trillium House
Wintergreen Dr., Devils Knob, Wintergreen Resort / P.O. Box 280, Nellysford, VA 22958
(804) 325-9126
Ed & Betty Dinwiddie
$65.00 to $150.00

Full breakfast
12 rooms, 12 private baths
Children allowed
No pets
Restricted smoking
Mastercard & Visa

Old-fashioned inn built to modern specifications. Large, noteworthy Oriental rugs in spacious common rooms and 5000+ volume library. Gourmet dinners served on weekends by reservation. Several bird feeders visible from the dining room windows.

CHEESE MUFFINS

3 cups sifted flour
2 1/2 teaspoons baking powder
1/4 cup sugar
1/2 teaspoon salt

1 egg, well-beaten
1 cup milk
1/4 cup shortening, melted
1 cup shredded cheese

Sift first four ingredients into mixing bowl. Add mixture of egg, milk, shortening and cheese. Stir only until moistened. Grease muffin pans on botton only. Fill cups 2/3 full. Bake at 400° for twenty minutes. Makes 12 muffins.

Submitted by:

Red Shutter Farmhouse
Route 1, Box 376
New Market, VA 22844
(703) 740-4281
George & Juanita Miller

Full breakfast
5 rooms, 5 private baths
Children allowed
No pets
Restricted smoking
Mastercard & Visa

Home located in the heart of the Shenandoah Valley at the foot of Massanutten Mountain on 20 acres, circa 1790, and enlarged about 1870, 1920 and 1930. Variety of large rooms and suites with queen or twin beds.

HERB POPOVERS

3/4 cup all-purpose flour
1/2 teaspoon celery salt
2 large eggs
1 cup milk
1 tablespoon butter, melted
2 tablespoons chopped fresh mixed herbs (such as chervil, parsley, chives and tarragon)

Generously grease 12 cup muffin pan. Sift flour and celery salt into a large bowl. Add eggs, milk and butter, and beat well. Stir in mixed herbs. Pour mixture into greased muffin cups. Place in cold oven, set temperature at 425° and bake 30 minutes without opening oven door. Makes 6 servings.

Submitted by:

The Country Fare B&B
402 N. Main Street
Woodstock, VA 22664
(703) 459-4828
Bette Hallgren
$45.00 to $65.00

Continental plus breakfast
3 rooms, 1 private bath
Children allowed
No pets
Restricted smoking
Visa

One of the oldest homes in the Shenandoah Valley, built in the late 18th century, with an addition in 1840. Used as a hospital from 1861 - 1864. Hand stenciling in original designs, filled with Grandmother's antiques and country collectibles. Sitting porch off the upstairs hall is the perfect spot to unwind on fair weather evenings.

MISS MARGUERITE'S BLUEBERRY OAT MUFFINS

3/4 cup Quaker Oats
1 1/2 cups flour
1 cup sugar
2 teaspoons baking powder
1 teaspoon salt
1 stick butter

Topping:
2 teaspoons sugar

1 1/2 teaspoons grated lemon rind
1 cup blueberries (preferably frozen) coated with 2 teaspoons flour
2/3 cup milk
1 egg, slightly beaten

1 1/2 teaspoons cinnamon

Preheat oven to 400°. Grind oatmeal into coarse powder. Combine with flour, sugar, baking powder and salt. Cut the butter and lemon rind into the dry ingredients with a pastry blender until the consistency is of coarse-looking meal. Add the flour-coated frozen blueberries and mix. In separate bowl, combine the milk and egg, then add to the dry ingredients. Stir just until dry ingredients are moistened. Batter will be thick and lumpy. Divide batter into 2 greased muffin pans. Sprinkle with sugar/cinnamon topping. Bake 20 - 25 minutes. Makes 12 muffins.

Submitted by:

Cedar Grove
Rte. 1, Box 2535, Fleeton Rd.
Reedville, VA 22539
(804) 453-3915
Susan & Bob Tipton
$60.00 to $80.00

Full breakfast
3 rooms, 1 private bath
No children
No pets
Restricted smoking

Gracious turn-of-the-century inn, featuring fine Victorian antiques and accommodations for the discerning traveller. Suite has balcony with panoramic view of Chesapeake Bay. Tennis on our court, sunbathe on our small beach, or borrow bikes for countryside ride. Breakfast served on fine china in formal dining room.

MONTEGO BAY MUFFINS

2 cups grated carrots
1/2 cup diced, peeled apple
1/2 cup raisins, soaked in hot water
1/2 cup chopped walnuts or pecans
1/2 cup flaked coconut
1 cup granulated sugar
1/4 cup brown sugar
1/2 cup softened margarine
3 eggs
2 teaspoons vanilla
1 1/2 cups all-purpose flour
1/2 cup All Bran cereal
2 teaspoons baking powder
1 teaspoon cinnamon
1/2 teaspoon salt

Combine carrots, apple, raisins, nuts and coconut; set aside. In large bowl, beat together sugars, margarine, eggs and vanilla; set aside. In another bowl, combine flour, bran cereal, baking powder, cinnamon and salt. Add carrot mixture and mix well. Add the sugar mixture and combine just until the flour is moistened. Spoon batter into 12 greased muffin cups and bake for 25 - 30 minutes in preheated 350° oven or until they test done. These muffins freeze well. Paper muffin cup liners make removal easier. Makes 12 muffins.

Submitted by:

West-Bocock House
1107 Grove Ave.
Richmond, VA 23220
(804) 358-6174
Mr. & Mrs. James B. West, Jr.
$65.00 to $75.00

Full breakfast
3 rooms, 3 private baths
Children allowed
No pets
Restricted smoking

Greek Revival home, circa 1871, on National Register, and in the Fan Area Historic District. Traditional Southern breakfast served in dining room or on verandah. American and English antiques, French linens and fresh flowers. Virginia Room boasts four-poster bed, fireplace, and sunporch overlooking the garden. TV in room.

POPPY SEED MUFFINS

2 cups all-purpose flour
2 teaspoons baking powder
1/2 teaspoon baking soda
3 tablespoons poppy seeds
1/4 cup sugar

1 cup lemon low-fat yogurt
1/3 cup melted butter
2 eggs
1 tablespoon lemon extract (or lemon juice)

In large bowl combine flour, baking powder, baking soda, poppy seeds, and sugar. In another bowl combine yogurt, butter, eggs and lemon extract or juice. Preheat oven to 375°. Grease muffin tins or use muffin paper liners. Add liquid ingredients to dry ingredients all at once. Stir until just combined. Put batter into muffin tin. Bake 20 minutes. This recipe freezes well and is easily doubled. Makes 12 muffins.

Submitted by:

L'Arche Farm Bed & Breakfast
1867 Mt. Tabor Road
Blacksburg, VA 24060
(703) 951-1808
Vera G. Good
$70.00

Full breakfast
3 rooms, 3 private baths
Children, over 12
No pets
No smoking

1790 farmhouse on 5 tranquil acres in Southwest VA. Visit New River Valley, VA Tech, and Radford University. Family heirlooms and antiques, with exposed beams from the original log home in the bedrooms. Good food and gracious hospitality are our trademark!

SAUSAGE MUFFINS

1/2 lb. bulk pork sausage
1/3 cup chopped green onions
1 cup biscuit mix (Bisquick or your choice)
1/2 teaspoon dry mustard
1/2 teaspoon ground red pepper
1/2 cup milk
1/2 cup finely shredded medium sharp Cheddar cheese

Combine sausage and green onions in a skillet; cook over medium heat until sausage is browned, stirring to crumble. Do not allow onions to burn or brown. Drain off all fat. Combine biscuit mix, dry mustard and red pepper. Add milk, stirring just until moistened. Stir in sausage mixture and cheese. Mixture will be thick. Spoon into greased muffin pans, filling 2/3 full. Bake at 400° for 15 minutes, or until muffins are golden. Do not overcook. Remove from pans immediately, serve warm. Makes 8 large muffins, 2 1/2 dozen miniature muffins.

Submitted by:

Bray's Manor
Route 3, Box 210
Hillsville, VA 24343
(703) 728-7901
Dick & Helen Bray
$42.60 to $53.25

Full breakfast
4 rooms, 2 private baths
Children allowed
No pets
Restricted smoking
Mastercard, Visa, Discover

Fine old home constructed shortly after the turn of the century. Rambling porch offers sitting, sipping, chatting and cool breezes Spring through Fall. Parlor and sitting rooms provide TV, books, cards, or VCR, before a warm fire in season.

SOUR CREAM MUFFINS

1 Duncan Hines butter cake mix
1/2 cup sugar
2 tablespoons brown sugar
1 teaspoon cinnamon
1/2 cup oil
1 cup sour cream
4 eggs
1 cup chopped nuts
1 teaspoon vanilla

Mix all ingredients together. Put into greased muffin tins, or in paper muffin liners. Bake at 350° for 20 minutes. Makes 2 dozen muffins.

Submitted by:

Hite's B&B
704 Monumental Avenue
Wiliamsburg, VA 23185
(804) 229-4814
James & Faye Hite
$50.00 to $65.00

Continental plus breakfast
2 rooms, 1 private bath
Children allowed
No pets
Restricted smoking

Attractive Cape Cod, just a 7-minute walk to Colonial Williamsburg. Large rooms furnished in collectibles and antiques. Guest rooms have phone, TV, radio and coffee maker, also a charming sitting area making breakfast a "private affair."

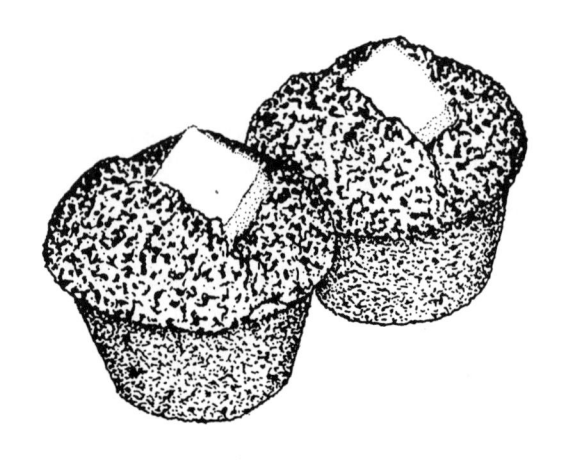

FRENCH TOAST, PANCAKES & WAFFLES

APPLE-OAT BRAN PANCAKES

1 cup oat bran cereal
   (hot, uncooked)
1 cup wheat flour
1 1/2 teaspoons baking
   powder
1/2 teaspoon salt
1 tablespoon sugar

2 teaspoons cinnamon
4 egg whites, beaten
1 1/2 cups apple juice
3 tablespoons melted
   shortening
1 large grated apple

Combine dry ingredients. Add beaten egg whites, apple juice, shortening and grated apple. Mix until slightly lumpy. Bake on moderately hot griddle, turning only once. Garnish with pecan halves and serve with apple syrup. Makes 10 - 12 pancakes.

Submitted by:

Needmoor Inn
801 Virginia Avenue
P.O. Box 629
Clarksville, VA 23927
(804) 374-2866
Lucy & Buddy Hairston
$45.00 to $55.00

Full breakfast
3 rooms, 3 private baths

Heartfelt hospitality, healthy gourmet breakfasts, and comfortable antique furnishings beckon the traveler to this 1889 Victorian B&B. Added amenities include the offerings of a mini-spa: therapeutic massage, luxurious facial care and herbal body treatments.

APPLE RAISIN NUT PUFFS

4 eggs
1 cup flour
Dash of nutmeg
1 cup skim milk
4 apples, peeled & chopped
1/4 cup raisins

1/4 cup chopped walnuts
Cinnamon & sugar to taste
4 tablespoons sunflower margarine
Powdered sugar
Maple syrup

Beat eggs, add flour, nutmeg, and milk. Mix until blended (batter will still be a little lumpy). In separate bowl combine apples, raisins, and nuts, and sprinkle with sugar and cinnamon to taste. Preheat oven to 400°. Put 1 tablespoon margarine in each of four au gratin dishes and place into the hot oven. Allow butter to melt, and dishes to get very hot (5 - 10 minutes). Remove from oven and pour 1/2 cup of batter into each of the dishes. Top with fruit mixture. Bake 15 - 20 minutes, until golden and puffy. Dust with powdered sugar. Serve immediately with Virginia maple syrup. Makes 4 servings.

Submitted by:

The Manor at Taylor's Store
Route 1, Box 533
Smith Mountain Lake, VA 24184
(703) 721-3951
Lee & Mary Lynn Tucker
$70.00 to $95.00

Full breakfast
6 rooms, 4 private baths, plus separate 3-bedroom cottage
Children allowed in cottage
No pets
No smoking
Mastercard & Visa

Explore this historic 120 acre estate and enjoy swimming, fishing, and canoeing in one of six private, spring-fed ponds. Porches, fireplaces, hot tub, billiard room, exercise room, guest kitchen, & large screen TV with movies. Hot air balloon rides also offered here!

EGGNOG WAFFLES

2 cups baking mix
  (biscuit mix)
1/4 teaspoon ground
  nutmeg

2 tablespoons salad oil
1 1/2 cups commercial
  eggnog *
1 egg

In a bowl, combine baking mix, nutmeg, salad oil, eggnog and egg; beat until smooth. Bake waffles in a preheated waffle iron according to manufacturer's directions. * Note: Purchase refrigerated eggnog when available, and freeze for as long as 2 months in original carton. Thaw in refrigerator and stir before using. Or may use canned eggnog. Makes 8 - 4" square waffles.

Submitted by:

Fleetwood Farm B&B
Route 1, Box 306-A
Leesburg, VA 22075
(703) 327-4325
Carol & Bill Chamberlin
$95.00 to $120.00

Full breakfast
2 rooms, 2 private baths, one
  with jacuzzi
Children, over 12
No pets
Restricted smoking

1745 historic landmark in VA hunt country. Antique-filled rooms, working fireplaces, and air-conditioning. Fluffy robes, candy, and flowers in rooms. Beautiful Colonial herb garden & grounds. Croquet, horseshoes, cook-out facilities. Working sheep farm.

GINGERBREAD PANCAKES

2 1/2 cups all-purpose flour
1 teaspoon baking powder
1 teaspoon baking soda
1/2 teaspoon salt
1 1/2 teaspoons ground cinnamon
1 1/2 teaspoons ground ginger
1 teaspoon ground nutmeg
1/8 - 1/4 teaspoon ground cloves
3 eggs
1/4 cup firmly packed brown sugar
1 cup buttermilk
1 cup water
1/4 cup brewed coffee
1/4 cup butter or margarine, melted

Combine first 8 ingredients, mix well. Combine eggs and sugar, beating well. Add buttermilk, water, coffee, and butter, mix well. Add buttermilk mixture to dry ingredients, stirring until just moistened (will be slightly lumpy). For each pancake, pour about 1/4 cup of batter onto a hot, lightly greased griddle. Turn when tops are covered with bubbles and edges appear slightly dry. Serve with warm applesauce or maple syrup. At Lambsgate, these pancakes are served with peach or strawberry sauce when in season. Makes 18 pancakes.

Submitted by:

Lambsgate Bed & Breakfast
Route 1, Box 63
Swoope, VA 24479
Location: Staunton, VA
(703) 337-6929
Dan & Elizabeth Fannon
$35.00 to $45.00

Full breakfast
3 rooms
Children allowed
No pets
No smoking

Restored 1816 vernacular brick farmhouse 6 miles west of historic Staunton. Comfortable, cozy lodging, bountiful Southern breakfast, and spectacular views of the Alleghenies. Surrounded by 7 pastoral acres with sheep and lambs. Relax, or hike or bike scenic back roads.

ORANGE YOGURT PANCAKES

1 1/4 cups Bisquick
1 tablespoon sugar
1 teaspoon grated
　orange rind
3/4 cup plain yogurt

1/3 cup orange juice
2 tablespoons melted
　butter, cooled
1 egg, slightly beaten
Fruit toppings of choice

Mix dry ingredients in medium size bowl. Mix remaining ingredients in smaller bowl. Combine with dry. Add extra splash of orange juice for slightly thinner, more workable batter. Fry on hot griddle. Top with sliced oranges, kiwi, bananas, strawberries, or a combination of all of these. Serves 3.

Submitted by:

The Inn at Monticello
Route 19, Box 112
Charlottesville, VA 22902
(804) 979-3593
Carol Engel & Alex Adams
$95.00 to $125.00

Full breakfast
5 rooms, 5 private baths
Children, over 8
No pets
No smoking
Mastercard & Visa

Warm hospitality, in 19th century manor, near restaurants and shops. Tastefully appointed, air-conditioned rooms filled with antiques/fine reproductions, some private porches, fireplaces, draped canopy beds. Guests love our country gourmet breakfasts!

PEANUT BUTTER WAFFLES

1 cup whole wheat flour
1/2 teaspoon salt
2 teaspoons baking powder
2 eggs, beaten
1/4 cup honey
1/2 teaspoon vanilla
1/2 cup peanut butter
1 1/4 cups milk

Stir together flour, salt and baking powder. In separate bowl, beat eggs, honey, vanilla and peanut butter. Then mix in the milk. Add the liquid mixture to the dry and stir until the ingredients are smooth. Bake on a hot, oiled waffle iron. Makes 4 waffles.

Submitted by:

Thornrose House
531 Thornrose Ave.
Staunton, VA 24401
(703) 885-7026
Otis & Suzanne Huston
$50.00 to $65.00

Full breakfast
5 rooms, 5 private baths
Children allowed
No pets
No smoking

Turn-of-the-century Georgian residence with wraparound verandah and Greek colonnades. Fireplace and grand piano create a formal, but comfortable, atmosphere. Bedrooms are on the second floor. Located adjacent to 300-acre park with tennis, golf, walks, and ponds.

SOUR CREAM WAFFLES WITH PEACHES

3 eggs, separated
3/4 cup milk
1/2 cup melted butter
1 teaspoon vanilla
3/4 cup sour cream
1 1/2 cups flour
2 teaspoons baking powder
1/2 teaspoon baking soda
1/2 teaspoon nutmeg
1/2 teaspoon salt
Topping:
3 fresh peaches (if possible), peeled, sliced and cooked
3/4 cup brown sugar
2 tablespoons butter
1/2 teaspoon nutmeg
1 tablespoon cornstarch

Beat egg yolks in large bowl. Beat in milk, melted butter, vanilla and sour cream. Combine flour, baking powder, soda, nutmeg and salt. Sift into egg mixture and beat well. Beat egg whites until stiff in separate bowl, fold into batter. Cook peeled, sliced peaches gently with brown sugar, butter and nutmeg. Add cornstarch to thicken at end of cooking time. Bake 4 - 5 tablespoons of batter per waffle in hot Belgian waffle iron for 1 minute and 40 seconds. Serve hot with warm peaches and butter. Have platter warm and serve at once. Makes 6 - 8 servings.

Submitted by:

Azalea House Bed & Breakfast
551 South Main St.
Woodstock, VA 22664
(703) 459-3500
Price & Margaret McDonald
$45.00 to $65.00

Full breakfast
3 rooms, 1 private bath
Children, over 10
No pets
Restricted smoking
Mastercard, Visa, Am Ex

100 year old Victorian house in North Shenandoah Valley with family antiques, lace curtains, balcony, porches, decks, and 5-course breakfast with candles and silver. Fresh flowers/afternoon tea and hot nut bread. Close to caverns, horseback & hiking trails, Civil War sites, and mountain views.

STUFFED FRENCH TOAST

1 loaf unsliced cinnamon bread
3 oz. soft cream cheese
Orange marmalade
4 eggs
1 cup milk
1 tablespoon sugar
1/4 teaspoon salt
1/2 teaspoon cinnamon
1 teaspoon vanilla
Butter for frying
Fresh strawberries, sliced & sugared
Syrup

Cut bread into 1" slices. Cut a "pocket" in each slice (across top and down side). Spread cream cheese and then marmalade inside. Dip into batter of eggs, milk, sugar, salt, cinnamon and vanilla. Fry in butter. Slice on angle to serve. Top with strawberries. Serve with syrup, scrambled eggs and bacon. Makes 8 servings.

Submitted by:

Liberty Rose B&B
1022 Jamestown Road
Williamsburg, VA 23185
(804) 253-1260
Brad & Sandi Hirz
$95.00 to $155.00

Full breakfast
4 rooms, 4 private baths
Children, over 10
No pets
No smoking
Mastercard & Visa

Affectionately referred to as "Williamsburg's most romantic B&B", on wooded hilltop near historic area. Grand puffy queen poster beds, vintage reproduction fabrics, silk & goose down bed coverings. In-room TV-VCR-movies, fireplaces, antiques, marble showers, porcelain clawfooted tubs. Highest reviews by ABBA, Fodors, AAA.

TRULY ELEGANT FRENCH TOAST

4 teaspoons sugar
1/4 teaspoon ground cinnamon
4 large eggs
1/2 cup half & half or cream
1 teaspoon vanilla extract
4 croissants
1 - 2 tablespoons butter

In a bowl mix sugar and cinnamon. Whisk in eggs, half & half or cream, and vanilla. Cut croissants in half horizontally, and dip in egg mixture. In frying pan or on griddle, melt butter over medium heat. Add croissants, and brown on both sides. Serve immediately - sprinkled with powdered sugar. Makes 4 servings.

Submitted by:

Ravenswood Inn
P.O. Box 250
Poplar Grove Lane
Mathews, VA 23109
(804) 725-7272
Marshall & Linda Warner
$70.00 to $85.00

Full breakfast
6 rooms, 5 private baths
No children
No pets
Restricted smoking

Romantic hideaway on Chesapeake's East River. Four acres surrounded by water. Restored 1913 manor home. Sailing charters on 30' sailboat available from Ravenswood pier. Outstanding for biking, flat, with no traffic. Hot tub.

Ravenswood Inn

BREADS

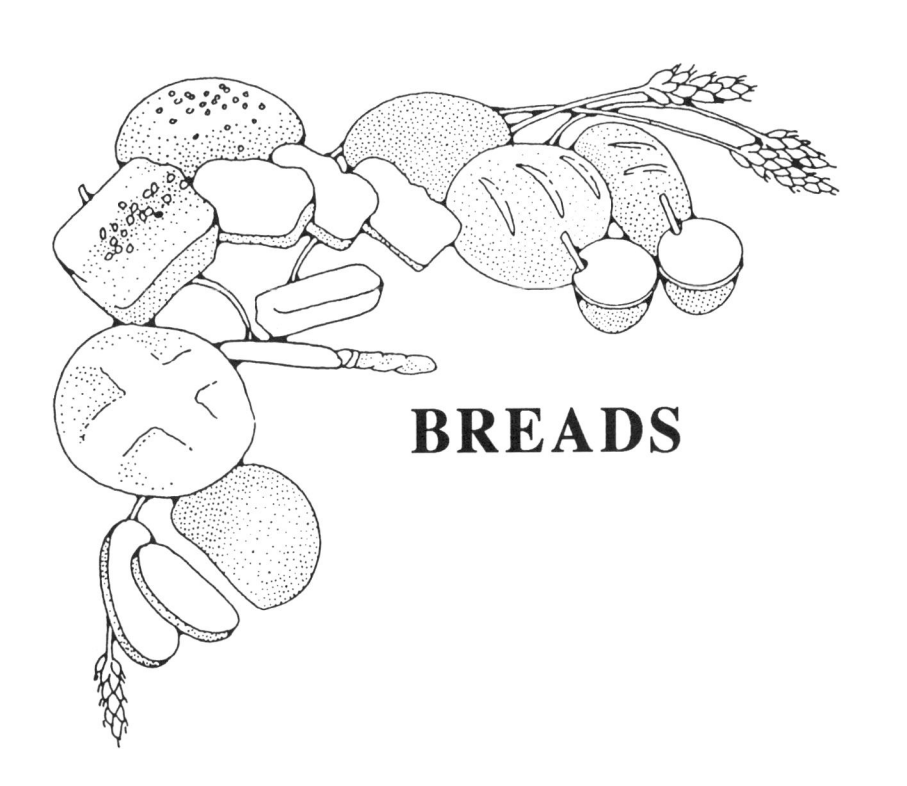

BREAD BIRDS

2 1/2 - 3 1/4 cups all-purpose flour
1/4 cup sugar
1 teaspoon salt
1 tablespoon dry yeast
1/2 cup milk
1/2 cup water
1/4 cup butter or margarine
1/2 teaspoon almond extract
1 egg
Currants & slivered almonds

Honey Butter Glaze:
Equal parts of honey and butter

Combine 1 cup flour, sugar, salt and yeast in large bowl. Mix well. Heat milk, water and butter to 130°. Add warm liquid to flour mixture and stir. Add almond extract and egg. Beat until smooth. Gradually add additional flour to make a soft dough. Knead until smooth and elastic. Place dough in greased bowl. Cover with plastic wrap and let rise about 45 minutes. Punch down and divide into 12 - 14 pieces. To shape birds, form each piece into a 10" roll and tie in a knot. Make 3 cuts in one end of knot to make tail feathers. Tuck in other end of knot to form a round head shape. Put on baking sheet and let rise in warm place for 25 minutes. Bake at 375° for 14 - 18 minutes, or until golden brown. Mix glaze and brush over birds immediately after baking. Return to oven for additional 3 - 4 minutes. Use potato nail to make 3 holes in bird's head, insert almond for beak and currants for eyes. Makes 12 - 14 birds.

Submitted by:

The Iris Inn
191 Chinquapin Drive
Waynesboro, VA 22980
(703) 943-1991
Wayne & Iris Karl
$75.00 to $85.00

Full breakfast
7 rooms, 7 private baths
Children limited
No pets
No smoking
Mastercard & Visa

Built in 1991 on 20-acre wooded tract on a western slope of the Blue Ridge. Spacious rooms with individual temperature controls. Views, porches, tower, great room, hot tub. Wildlife and nature themes. Just off I-64, Exit 96.

FAMILY FRUIT LOAF

1 cup sugar
1 cup milk
1 cup raisins
1/4 lb. butter or
　margarine

1 egg
2 cups self-rising flour
1/2 teaspoon baking
　powder
Chopped nuts (optional)

Mix together sugar, milk, raisins and butter in a large saucepan and heat until butter is melted. Do not boil. Set aside to cool. When cool, add egg and blend. Slowly add flour, baking powder, and nuts, if desired. Pour into loaf pan and bake for 1 hour at 350°. Makes 10 - 12 servings.

Submitted by:

Danscot House
P.O. Box 157
Palmyra, VA 22963
(804) 589-1977
Sven & Connie Pedersen
$50.00 to $70.00

Full breakfast
3 rooms, 1 + 1 private baths
Children allowed
No pets
Restricted smoking

What makes us special is that we are not a hotel or an inn. This is our home, and we try to create an atmosphere of being a house guest, rather than a commercialized customer. It is quiet, private and relaxed. The food is also good!!!

GRANDMA'S COFFEE NUT BREAD

2 1/2 cups sifted flour
3 teaspoons baking powder
3/4 cup sugar
1/4 teaspoon salt
3/4 cup chopped walnuts
1 egg, beaten
1/2 cup double-strength coffee
1/2 cup evaporated milk

Sift and mix dry ingredients, stir in walnuts. Combine egg, coffee, and milk. Add to dry ingredients and mix well. Bake in loaf pan at 350° for one hour.

Submitted by:

Piney Grove at Southall's Plantation
P.O. Box 1359
Williamsburg, VA 23187
(804) 829-2480
Joseph & Joan Gordineer,
Brian Gordineer
$125.00 to $150.00

Full breakfast
6 rooms, 4 private baths
Children allowed
No pets
No smoking

Historic landmark, and National Register property located 20 miles west of Williamsburg in the James River Plantation country. Working fireplaces, plantation breakfast, pool, nature trail, gardens, farm animals, and nearby historic sites and plantations. Gracious hospitality and elegant accommodations from VA's past await you.

HERB BREAD

1 pkg. active dry yeast
1/4 cup warm water
2 tablespoons sugar
2 tablespoons shortening
1 1/2 teaspoons salt
3/4 cup milk, scalded
3 - 3 1/2 cups sifted all-purpose flour
1/4 teaspoon nutmeg
1/4 teaspoon onion powder
1/2 teaspoon ground sage
1 teaspoon ground celery seed
1 egg, slightly beaten

Soften yeast in warm water, set aside. Combine next 4 ingredients, cool to lukewarm. Add half of the flour, mix well. Add spices, yeast mixture and egg; beat until smooth. Add remaining flour, knead on floured surface until smooth. Place in lightly greased bowl, turn dough once, cover and let rise until double, about 1 1/2 hours. Punch down, cover and let rest 10 - 15 minutes. Shape into round loaf, place in greased 8" or 9" pie plate. Cover and let rise until almost double in size, about 1 hour. Bake at 400° for 35 minutes. Makes 1 loaf.

Submitted by:

The Henry Clay Inn
114 N. Railroad Avenue
Ashland, VA 23005
(804) 798-3100
Carol C. Martin
$70.00 to $145.00

Full breakfast
15 rooms, 15 private baths
Children allowed
No pets
No smoking
Mastercard & Visa

Old-time southern charm in historic Victorican town: from fireplaces, to rocking chairs on the grand front porch. Enjoy Restaurant's family style meals, Art Gallery and Gift Gallery. Drawing room is perfect for receptions, meetings, reunions or luncheons. Entertainment and historic sites nearby.

PUMPKIN CURRANT LOAF

1 1/4 cups sugar (can be reduced to 1 cup + 2 tablespoons)
1/2 cup canola oil
2 eggs
1 cup unseasoned pumpkin
1 3/4 cups all-purpose unbleached flour
3/4 teaspoon salt
1 teaspoon baking soda
1/2 teaspoon ground cloves
1 teaspoon cinnamon
1 teaspoon allspice
1/2 teaspoon freshly grated nutmeg
1/3 cup water
1/2 cup currants

Preheat oven to 350°. Combine sugar and oil. Stir in eggs and pumpkin. Combine all dry ingredients. Sift dry ingredients into pumpkin mixture, alternating water, and dry ingredients. Fold in currants. Pour into greased and lightly floured loaf pan/pans. Bake about 1 hour or until tester comes out clean. This loaf always bakes perfectly with a moist, tender texture, and not too sweet flavor. Best to bake it the day before serving. Freezes extremely well, as texture stays moist. Makes 1 - 9" x 5" loaf or 3 - 5" x 3" loaves.

Submitted by:

The Sampson Eagon Inn
238 East Beverley St.
Staunton, VA 24401
(703) 886-8200
Frank & Laura Mattingly
$75.00 to $85.00

Full breakfast
4 rooms, 4 private baths
Children, over 12
No pets
No smoking

Warm hospitality, attentive personal service and classic elegance of an antebellum mansion create unique experience in historic lodging. Scrumptious breakfasts, spacious a/c accommodations, romantic canopied beds and period decor. Adjacent to Woodrow Wilson birthplace and Mary Baldwin College. Near dining and antiquing.

THISTLE HILL RAISIN BREAD

1 cup milk, scalded
3/4 cup sugar
1 teaspoon salt
1/4 cup butter
1/2 cup lukewarm water
2 pkgs. dry yeast
4 1/2 cups flour
1 cup raisins
4 eggs, lightly beaten
Cinnamon to taste
1/4 cup chopped almonds

Combine milk, sugar, salt and butter in large mixing bowl and stir until butter is melted. Cool to lukewarm. Pour the warm water into a small warm bowl and sprinkle yeast over water, then stir gently until yeast is dissolved. Stir into milk mixture. Combine 1/4 cup flour with raisins and set aside. Add eggs and 2 cups flour to yeast mixture and beat until smooth. Add remaining flour and mix well. Cover and let rise in a warm place until doubled in bulk. Punch down dough, then add raisins and knead into dough. Grease two loaf pans, sprinkle with cinnamon. Scatter almonds over bottom of pans. Pour dough into pans. Cover and let rise for 1 hour or until double in bulk. Bake in preheated 350° oven for 45 minutes or until loaves test done. Cool for 10 minutes, then remove from pans onto wire rack. Excellent lightly toasted! Makes 2 loaves.

Submitted by:

Thistle Hill Bed & Breakfast
Route 1, Box 291
Boston, VA 22713
(703) 987-9142
Charles & Marianne Wilson
$80.00 to $135.00

Full breakfast
4 rooms, 4 private baths
No pets
Restricted smoking
Mastercard & Visa

Old world comfort and modern amenities in Blue Ridge Foothills. Colonial style home decorated in period furnishings. Candlelight dinners by reservation, fireplaces, air-conditioning, hot tub. Near Skyline Drive and Washington, VA.

EGG, MEAT
&
CHEESE DISHES

APPLE RAISIN QUICHE

Pastry for one 9" pie crust

3 3/4 cups Granny Smith apples, peeled, cored and sliced

1/2 cup raisins

1/4 cup packed brown sugar

2 teaspoons cinnamon

3 cups shredded Monterey Jack cheese

3 eggs

1 cup whipping cream

Preheat oven to 400°. Line a 9" pie plate with pastry. Crimp edge and prick bottom and sides with a fork. Bake 16 minutes. Line with aluminum foil to prevent shrinkage. Remove from oven. Layer half of the apples, raisins, brown sugar and cinnamon into pie shell. Repeat layers. Cover with cheese. Beat eggs with cream. Make a small hole in cheese and pour in egg mixture. Cover hole with cheese. Bake for 1 hour at 400°. Cool 15 minutes before cutting. Makes 8 servings.

Submitted by:

Frederick House
18 East Frederick Street
Staunton, VA 24401
(800) 334-5575 or
Joe & Evy Harman
$45.00 to $95.00

Full breakfast
14 rooms, 14 private baths
Children allowed
No pets
No smoking
Mastercard, Visa, Am Ex, Discover

A small hotel across from Mary Baldwin College, in Staunton, the oldest city in the Shenandoah Valley. Together with us on Frederick Street are Chumley's Tearoom, the Town Center Athletic Club, and McCormick's Restaurant. Breakfast is served at Chumley's, lunch and dinner at McCormick's. Swim in the Town Center.

ASPARAGUS CRUSTLESS QUICHE

10 eggs
1/2 cup flour
1 teaspoon baking powder
1/2 teaspoon salt
2 cups cottage cheese

4 cups shredded white Cheddar cheese
1/2 cup melted butter or oleo (1 stick)
1 lb. asparagus (washed, cut into 1" pieces, with tough ends broken off)
Paprika to taste

Beat eggs until light in large bowl. Add flour, baking powder, salt, cottage cheese, Cheddar cheese, butter and asparagus. Mix well. Pour into buttered 9" x 13" pan. Sprinkle paprika on top. Bake at 350° for 35 - 40 minutes. Cut into squares. Makes 10 servings.

Submitted by:

Oak Grove Plantation
P.O. Box 45
Cluster Springs, VA 24535
(804) 575-7137
Pickett Craddock
$45.00 to $50.00

Full breakfast
2 rooms
Children allowed
No pets
Restricted smoking

Operated May to September by Pickett Craddock, a descendant of the 1820 builders. Breakfast served with Southern hospitality in Victorian dining room. Hiking, biking on 400 acre grounds. Nearby are Buggs Island Lake, and historic Danville. Children welcomed.

BREAKFAST SOUFFLÉ FOR HEARTY APPETITES

12 slices coarse-grained white bread, crust removed	4 eggs, slightly beaten
	1/2 teaspoon dry mustard
6 slices thin American cheese	2 cups milk
	1/3 cup butter or margarine, melted
6 slices thin Virginia ham	
6 slices thin Swiss cheese	2/3 cup Corn Flakes, crushed

Grease a 9" x 13" x 2" Pyrex baking dish. Arrange 4 slices of bread at corners of dish and 4 half slices of bread in middle of dish. Top bread with American cheese, then ham, then Swiss, and cover with remaining bread, in the same arrangement as the bottom slices. Beat eggs and dry mustard, mixing well, and combine with milk. Pour over sandwiches. Cover and refrigerate overnight. Before baking, pour melted butter evenly over casserole, and sprinkle with Corn Flake crumbs. Bake in 350° oven for 55 - 60 minutes or until slightly brown and puffed. Cut into 4 servings, and serve at once. Present with garnish of melons and/or cluster of grapes. Makes 4 servings.

Submitted by:

Colonial Capital
  Bed & Breakfast
501 Richmond Road
Williamsburg, VA 23185-3537
(800) 776-0570
Barbara & Phil Craig
$90.00 to $125.00 (suite)

Full breakfast
5 rooms, 5 private baths
Children, over 6
No pets
Restricted smoking
Mastercard & Visa

Elegantly furnished Colonial Revival, circa 1926, only 3 blocks from historic area. Cozy canopy beds, and breakfast with class. Classic plantation parlor with woodburning fireplace, afternoon tea and wine. Complimentary bikes, off-street parking, central a/c, screened porch, patio and deck.

CRAB CASSEROLE Á LA GREENVALE

- 8 oz. crab meat
- 1 1/2 cups cubed Swiss cheese
- 1 medium onion, finely chopped
- 1 green pepper, chopped
- 1/2 teaspoon salt
- 1/4 teaspoon pepper
- Lemon juice to taste
- 1/4 cup mayonnaise
- Parmesan cheese to taste

Preheat oven to 350°. Mix crab, cheese, onion, and green pepper. Add salt and pepper. Add lemon juice to mayonnaise until thin enough to mix easily with crab mixture. Stir into crab mixture. Put into buttered baking dish. Bake for 30 minutes. Sprinkle Parmesan on top during last 5 minutes of baking. Makes 4 servings.

Submitted by:

Greenvale Manor
Route 354, Box 70
Mollusk, VA 22517
(804) 462-5995
Pam & Walt Smith
$65.00 to $95.00

Full breakfast
6 rooms, 6 private baths
No children
No pets
Restricted smoking
Mastercard & Visa

Romantic, relaxing 1840 Waterfront plantation, with sweeping views of Rappahannock River & Greenvale Creek. Antiques, a/c, fireplaces in 2 suites. Beach, pool, dock, bicycles, and boats for rent. Watch a river sunset from our verandah & unwind on 13 acres of rural privacy.

DIXIELAND SAUSAGE-RICE CASSEROLE

1/2 - 1 lb. bulk sausage
1 cup onion, chopped
1 cup celery, chopped
1/2 cup green pepper, chopped
1/8 teaspoon pepper (or use hot sausage)
1/2 teaspoon garlic powder
1/4 teaspoon salt
1 cup rice, uncooked (white or converted)
1 can cream of mushroom soup
1 can cream of chicken soup
1 can water

Crumble up sausage and brown in a big frying pan. Pour off the grease. Add onion, celery, and green pepper, black pepper, garlic powder, salt, rice, soup and water. Mix together and bake, tightly covered in 9" x 13" x 2" Pyrex baking dish at 350° for 1 1/2 hours. If convenient, after about 45 minutes cooking time, stir the mixture. After the allotted cooking time you may need to add some additional water to this casserole if the rice has become too dry. Just gradually pour in warm water and stir to moisten. Serves 6.

Submitted by:

Sims-Mitchell House B&B
242 Whittle St., P.O. Box 429
Chatham, VA 24531
(804) 432-0595 For reservations: 1-800-967-2867
Henry & Patricia Mitchell
$45.00 to $70.00

Full breakfast
2 suites, 2 private baths
Children allowed
No pets
No smoking
Mastercard & Visa

Historic 1870 home with family atmosphere, in charming Victorian town. Main house's raised English basement is spacious guest suite with 2 bedrooms, sitting room, & private entrance. Adjacent cottage suite has 2 bedrooms, sitting room & kitchen. Hostess is nationally-known cookbook writer; host, a planetarium specialist; both natives.

EASIEST TURKEY & HAM TIMBALES

- 2 oz. cubed turkey, ham or chicken
- 2 oz. June or sharp Cheddar cheese
- 2 or 3 eggs
- 1/2 cup milk
- 2 tablespoons chopped scallions
- 1/2 teaspoon paprika
- 1/2 teaspoon white pepper
- 1 teaspoon Parmesan cheese

Lightly grease 2 - 6 oz. custard cups and place cubed meat and shredded cheese on the bottom. Mix eggs, milk, scallions, paprika and pepper and pour half into each custard cup on top of the meat and cheese. Top with Parmesan cheese and bake in a 375° oven for 30 minutes. Serve hot. Makes 2 servings.

Submitted by:

High Meadows Vineyard Inn
Rte. 20 S.   Route 4, Box 6
Scottsville, VA 24590
(804) 286-2218
Peter Sushka & Jae Abbitt
$75.00 to $130.00

Full breakfast
12 rooms, 12 private baths
Children allowed
Pets allowed by prior arrangement
No smoking
Mastercard & Visa

19th century architectural two-period historic landmark evokes old-world ambience. Romantic gardens surround the inn, inviting you outdoors. Pastoral setting on 23 acres, relaxing walks, European evening supper baskets at the pond, gazebo or vineyard. Terrace & fireside breakfasting. Near Charlottesville, Monticello & Univ. of VA.

EGGS BENEDICT CALEDONIA

2 quality split English muffins
Butter or margarine
4 slices Canadian bacon or ham
4 eggs, poached
1 pkg. Hollandaise sauce mix
3 tablespoons lemon juice

Toast or broil muffin halves and spread with butter. Top with slices of Canadian bacon or ham. Warm at 160° in oven. Poach eggs for 3 1/2 minutes in cups sprayed with vegetable oil. With whites set and yolks liquid, place inverted eggs upon muffins. Prepare Hollandaise sauce replacing 3 tablespoons of water with lemon juice. Cover eggs with sauce. Garnish with fresh parsley, kiwi slice, strawberry half, or a favorite garnish of your choice. Practice this dish for confidence! Makes 2 servings.

Submitted by:

Caledonia Farm B&B
Route 1, Box 2080
Flint Hill, VA 22627
(703) 675-3693
Phil Irwin
$70.00 to $100.00

Full breakfast
2 rooms + 1 suite,
 1 private bath
Children, over 12
No pets
No smoking
Mastercard & Visa

National Register landmark adjacent to Shenandoah National Park. Beautifully restored 1812 stone home and romantic summer kitchen are surrounded by pasturelands and accented by 3,300' Blue Ridge Mtns. Working fireplaces, individual heat & a/c, Skyline Drive views, hayrides, porches, bicycles, lawn games. Evening dining nearby.

EXTRA SPECIAL SCRAMBLED EGGS

4 - 6 eggs
1/2 teaspoon West Indian hot sauce
1 1/2 tablespoons cream cheese, softened
1/2 cup cream (or milk)
1 tablespoon fresh chives, chopped
1 tablespoon butter

Beat eggs in bowl. Add remaining ingredients, except butter, and beat until well-blended. Melt butter in saucepan, then add egg mixture. Cook over medium heat, stirring constantly, until desired doneness. Serves 2 - 3 persons.

Submitted by:

Lavender Hill Farm
Route 631, RR# 1, Box 515
Lexington, VA 24450
(703) 464-5877 or
(800) 446-4240
Cindy & Colin Smith
$45.00 to $65.00

Full breakfast
3 rooms, 3 private baths
Children allowed
No pets
No smoking
Mastercard & Visa

English country charm and hospitality are combined with superb food to ensure a memorable stay. Located just over 4 miles from historic Lexington, on a working farm. Relax by the creek, or go for a walk and enjoy panoramic mountain views. Dinner is available to guests and is rapidly becoming the reason for many a repeat visit.

HERB-BAKED EGGS

- 1 tablespoon butter
- 4 large eggs
- 1 teaspoon prepared dijon mustard
- 1/3 - 1/2 cup plain (non-fat) yogurt
- 3/4 cup shredded Cheddar cheese
- 1 tablespoon chopped fresh chives
- 1 tablespoon chopped fresh parsley

Garnish:
Sprigs of herbs

Preheat oven to 350°. Butter 4 ramekins. In medium bowl, beat eggs, mustard and yogurt. Stir in 1/4 cup cheese. In small bowl, mix chives and parsley. Add 1/2 of the mixed herbs to the egg mixture. Stir well and spoon mixture into prepared ramekins. Sprinkle with the remaining cheese and herbs. Bake in a pan with about half an inch of water, for about 45 minutes, or until firm and golden. Turn out onto serving plates. Garnish with herbs.

Submitted by:

The Inn at the Crossroads
Route 2, Box 6   R.R. 692
North Garden, VA 22959
(804) 979-6452
Lynn Neville & Christine Garrison
$59.00 to $69.00

Full breakfast
5 rooms
Children, over 8
No pets
Restricted smoking (outside)
Mastercard & Visa

Newly renovated landmark tavern with cozy guest rooms and two sitting rooms. Breakfast is served in the original "Keeping Room." Homemade muffins & breads with jams and jellies and strawberry butter. Ideal location for enjoying the historic charm of Charlottesville, and the beauty of the Blue Ridge Mountains.

MILE HIGH QUICHE

Pastry for pie crust to fit bottom and sides of 9" springform pan
1/2 lb. sliced bacon
3 cups natural Swiss cheese, grated
6 whole eggs
1 egg yolk (save white to brush on crust)
1 1/4 teaspoons salt
1/8 teaspoon nutmeg
1/8 teaspoon freshly ground black pepper
Dash of cayenne pepper
3 cups light cream
2 green onions, chopped

Preheat oven to 375°. Brush the pie crust with egg white. Fry the bacon until crisp, drain and crumble. Sprinkle bacon, then green onion over the bottom of crust. Sprinkle the grated cheese over the bacon and green onion. In a large bowl add whole eggs, egg yolk, salt, nutmeg, pepper, and cayenne, and beat lightly with a whisk or rotary beater. Gradually add cream, and beat mixture until well combined, but not frothy. Slowly pour the mixture over the bacon and cheese in the pie shell. Bake 50 - 55 minutes, or until top is a golden brown and puffy and the center seems firm when it is gently pressed with fingertips. Remove to a wire rack and let cool 15 minutes. With a sharp knife, loosen edge of pastry from side of pan, gently remove side of springform pan. Place, still on the bottom of pan, onto a serving plate. Serve warm. Makes 6 - 8 servings.

Submitted by:

Llewellyn Lodge
603 South Main St.
Lexington, VA 24450
(800) 882-1145
Ellen & John Roberts
$65.00 to $80.00

Full breakfast
6 rooms, 6 private baths
Children, over 10
No pets
Restricted smoking
Mastercard, Visa, Am Ex

Lexington's first established B&B is within walking distance of Historic District. Warm, friendly atmosphere offering country charm with a touch of class. Relax with afternoon refreshments. Gourmet breakfast brings many a repeat visitor. Near the Lee Chapel, Stonewall Jackson House, VMI and Washington & Lee University.

REDNECK SOUFFLÉ

2 lbs. frozen, Southern style hash browns
1/4 cup dried or 1/2 cup fresh minced onion
Granulated or fresh garlic, to taste
Lawry's® Pinch of Herbs & Mixed Peppers, to taste
Cayenne pepper (opt.)
1/2 lb. cooked, ground, lean country ham (or crumbled cooked bacon or corned beef) *
9 eggs, beaten
1/4 lb. crumbled Cheddar cheese
Sesame seeds to taste

Lightly oil a 12" skillet, then add potatoes and onion. Season liberally with Herbs and Peppers, garlic, and a dash of cayenne if desired. Fry over medium heat until potatoes begin to brown. Add meat and/or mushrooms & continue to cook, turning frequently. When potatoes are done, add eggs, lower heat. Quickly, mix thoroughly, pat into a firm cake shape away from sides of pan & cover. When eggs brown on bottom, flip, or turn into another 12" pan. Sprinkle Cheddar cheese over the "done" side, then sesame seeds. Cover until eggs are cooked through, then pie-slice into 8 pieces. Note: Proportion into a 10" pan for 6 slices, an 8" - 9" pan for 4 slices, or a 7" pan for 2 slices. *Mushrooms may be substituted for or added to the meat.

Submitted by:

The Osceola Mill Country Inn
Steele's Tavern, VA 24476
(703) 377-MILL (6455)

Full breakfast
11 rooms, 11 private baths & Honeymoon Cottage with bath
Children allowed
Pets considered
No smoking

A warm, friendly & unpretentious alternative to both hotels or motels and other inns. Charming accommodations, two parlors, music room, game room and dining room. Pool, porches and babbling brook for relaxation. Biking, hiking, antiquing, exploring, golf, & fishing nearby.

SAUSAGE-APPLE RING

2 eggs
1/2 cup milk
1 1/2 cups crushed
   saltine crackers

1 cup peeled, chopped
   apple
1/4 cup chopped onion
1/4 teaspoon pepper
2 lbs. bulk pork sausage

Beat together eggs and milk in bowl. Stir in crushed crackers, chopped apple, onion, and pepper. Add sausage, mix well. Lightly grease (or use thin spray of Pam), 6 1/2 cup ring mold. Firmly pat mixture into mold. Carefully unmold onto a rack in shallow baking pan. Bake at 350° for 50 minutes. Transfer to warm platter. Center can be filled with scrambled eggs. Makes 12 servings.

Submitted by:

Dulwich Manor
Route 5, Box 173A
Amherst, VA 24521
(804) 946-7207
Bob & Judy Reilly
$65.00 to $85.00

Full breakfast
6 rooms, 4 private baths
Children allowed
No pets
Restricted smoking

Stately English manor house surrounded by lush woods and meadows. Majestic Blue Ridge Mountain. view, near Washington National Forest, 22 miles from Blue Ridge Parkway. Relax in our steaming outdoor hot tub. Large charming bedchambers, whirlpool, bay window. Fireplaces, expansive columned verandah.

SPANOKOPITA (GREEK SPINACH AND CHEESE PIE)

1/2 pkg. (1 lb. size) phyllo leaves
1/2 cup margarine, melted
1/2 cup finely minced onion
3 pkgs. frozen chopped spinach, thawed and well-drained
3 eggs, slightly beaten
1/2 lb. feta cheese, crumbled
1/4 cup chopped parsley
2 tablespoons chopped fresh dill (or 1 tablespoon dried dill)
1/2 teaspoon black pepper
1 teaspoon salt

Preheat oven to 350°. Pastry must be at room temperature. Follow package directions. Melt margarine and set aside. Place all other ingredients in bowl and mix together until well blended. Brush a 13" x 9" x 2" baking pan lightly with melted margarine. In bottom of pan layer 8 phyllo leaves one by one, brushing top of each with melted margarine. Spread evenly with spinach mixture. Cover with 8 more leaves, brushing each with remaining margarine. Cut through top pastry layer on diagonal, then cut in opposite direction to form diamonds. Bake 30 - 35 minutes until top is golden brown. Makes up to 16 pieces.

Submitted by:

Firmstone Manor B&B Inn
Route 1, Box 257
Longdale Furnace Road
Clifton Forge, VA 24422
(703) 862-0892
Marko & Danica Diana Popin
$65.00 to $125.00

Full or continental breakfast
8 rooms, 4 private baths
Children allowed
No pets
No smoking
Mastercard & Visa

1873 English Victorian manor house set in yesteryear ambience, surrounded by Allegheny Mountains. Fine provincial Chef de Cuisine dining is as pleasing to the palate as the tasteful decor is to the eye. Decorated with emphasis on comfort and relaxation. Recreation and history abound in the area.

SPINACH AND CHEESE SQUARES

1 cup flour
1 teaspoon salt (opt.)
1 teaspoon baking powder
10 oz. frozen chopped spinach (thawed and squeezed dry)
2 eggs, beaten (room temperature)
1 cup milk
4 tablespoons melted butter or margarine
3/4 lb. shredded Cheddar cheese

Mix all ingredients together. Place in 9" x 9" greased metal pan. Bake 30 - 35 minutes in 350° oven. Loosen edges when removed from oven. Cool slightly, cut into squares. Freezes well. Reheat at 400° for 20 minutes or until heated through.

Submitted by:

Anderson Cottage B&B
Box 176
Warm Springs, VA 24484
(703) 839-2975
Jean Randolph Bruns
$55.00 to $110.00

Full breakfast
5 rooms, 4 private baths
Children allowed
Prefer no pets
Restricted smoking

Quiet mountain valley setting near Warm Springs Pools, the Homestead Hotel, hiking trails, and lake swimming. Rambling 18th/early 19th century home with spacious suites and rooms. Brick kitchen is independent 2-bedroom housekeeping unit.

SYCAMORE HILL HOUSE CINNAMON APPLE PUFF

1 very large tart apple
1/2 cup flour
1/2 cup whole milk
3 large eggs
1 teaspoon sugar
Dash of salt
2 tablespoons butter
1 tablespoon cinnamon sugar
Juice of 1 fresh lemon

Liberally grease a 9" fluted edge quiche dish. Core, peel, and thinly slice apple, and sauté in 1 tablespoon butter until tender. Spread apple slices evenly in the quiche dish. By hand, mix together flour, milk, eggs, sugar and salt until blended and pour over apple slices. Bake at 500° for 10 minutes. Remove from oven, dot with 1 tablespoon butter, sprinkle with cinnamon sugar. Return to the oven for 5 minutes. Bring to the table immediately, and pour juice of one lemon over the top. Serves 4 with accompaniments.

Submitted by:

Sycamore Hill House & Gardens
Route 1, Box 978
Washington, VA 22747
(703) 675-3046
Kerri & Stephen Wagner
$95.00 to $120.00

Full breakfast
3 rooms, 3 private baths
Children, over 12
No pets
No smoking
Mastercard & Visa

Certified wildlife sanctuary, spectacular Blue Ridge Mtn. views from a 65' wraparound verandah. Unique, contemporary inn, with 52 acres and beautiful gardens. Kerri's famous indoor flowers: exotic orchids and showy African violets, fill every corner. Steve is internationally-published illustrator; his work is displayed throughout the house.

ASSORTED
BAKED GOODS

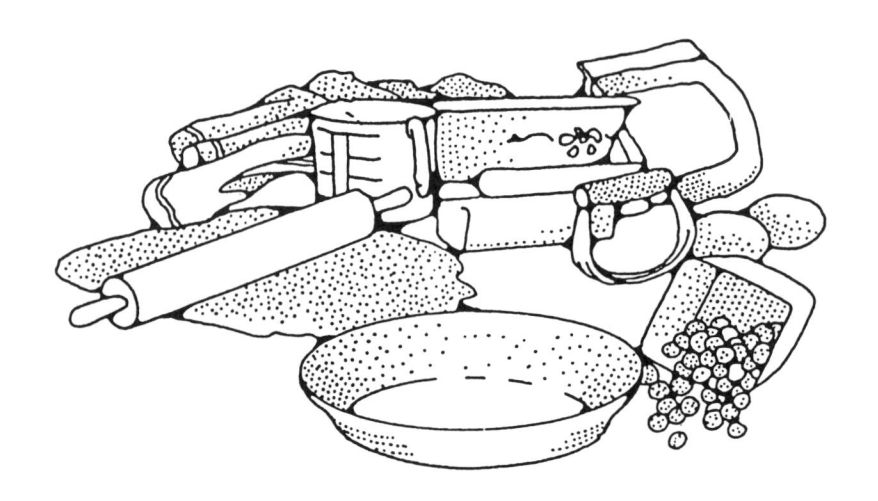

BUTTER BISCUITS

2 sticks frozen butter
4 1/2 cups self-rising
   flour

2 tablespoons sour
   cream
2 cups milk

Chip frozen butter into small pieces in a large bowl. Add flour, sour cream and milk. Stir until well combined. Dough will be very soft. With well-floured hands, pinch dough into biscuits and place on lightly greased cookie sheet. Bake at 400° for 10 - 15 minutes until lightly browned. Makes 18 - 20 biscuits.

Submitted by:

Winridge Bed & Breakfast
Route 1, Box 362
Madison Heights, VA 24572
(804) 384-7220
LoisAnn & Ed Pfister
$49.00 to $69.00

Full breakfast
3 rooms, 1 private bath
Children allowed
No pets
Restricted smoking

Grand, colonial southern home on peaceful country meadows. Wonderful mountain views. Swing under shade trees and stroll through gardens enjoying flowers, birds and butterflies that abound. Large, sunny windows and spacious rooms with high ceilings. Join our family for a warm welcome in a casual atmosphere.

COTTAGE CINNAMON BUNS

1/2 cup raisins
1/2 cup chopped pecans
1 pkg. small round frozen dough
1/2 pkg. butterscotch pudding

1 cup brown sugar
1/2 stick butter or oleo, melted
3/4 teaspoon cinnamon

Grease bundt pan. Sprinkle about half of raisins and nuts on bottom of pan. Place frozen dough balls loosely around pan and proceed to sprinkle the butterscotch pudding, brown sugar, remaining raisins and nuts, and cinnamon over and in between the dough. Pour melted butter over mixture. Cover and let rise overnight in cold oven. Bake in preheated 350° oven for 20 - 25 minutes. Makes 6 servings.

Submitted by:

Barclay Cottage
400 16th Street
Virginia Beach, VA 23451
(804) 422-1956
Peter & Claire
$65.00 to $80.00

Full breakfast
6 rooms, 3 private baths
No children
No pets
No smoking
Mastercard & Visa

Restored historical inn, two blocks from the beach and fishing pier. Located in the heart of Virginia Beach recreational area. We have tried to keep the ambience of the old inn, while modernizing it significantly to bring you the feeling of yesterday, with the comfort of today.

CREAM OF WHEAT CAKE

2 eggs
1 cup sugar
1/2 cup vegetable oil
1 cup milk
1 cup cream of wheat
2 tablespoons all-purpose flour
2 apples, peeled and shredded
1 1/2 teaspoons baking powder
1 cup walnuts

Whip eggs, sugar and oil. Set aside. Mix milk, cream of wheat, flour, shredded apples, and baking powder. Fold in the egg mixture. Add nuts. Grease and flour a 9" cake pan. Pour mixture in and bake one hour at 350°. Makes 4 servings.

Submitted by:

Erika's Cottage
706 Richmond Road
Williamsburg, VA 23185
(804) 229-6421
Erika & Walter Gerber
$85.00

Full breakfast
2 rooms, 2 private baths
Children, over 6
No pets
No smoking
Mastercard & Visa

Decor is a melange of antiques & art deco, mostly family treasures. Spacious, newly decorated rooms, double and queen beds, crisp bed sheets, down comforters, and adjacent sitting room with TV. Wake up to aroma of Erika's freshly baked breads. Breakfast served in a dining room with a view.

DRIED FRUIT CREAM SCONES

2 cups all-purpose flour
1 tablespoon baking powder
1/2 teaspoon salt
1/4 cup sugar

1/2 cup chopped dried fruit (apricots or prunes)
1/4 cup raisins
1 1/4 cups heavy cream

Glaze:
3 tablespoons sweet butter, melted

2 tablespoons sugar

Preheat oven to 425°. Combine flour, baking powder, salt and sugar. Mix well. Add dried fruit and raisins. Stir in cream, and mix with fork until dough holds together. Transfer dough to lightly floured board. Knead 8 or 9 times. Pat into circle 10" round. Brush with sweet butter and sprinkle top with sugar. Cut circle into 12 wedges. Place each wedge on ungreased baking sheet. Allow 1" between pieces. Bake 15 minutes or until golden brown. Makes 12 pieces.

Submitted by:

Page House Inn
323 Fairfax Avenue
Norfolk, VA 23507
(804) 625-5033
Stephanie & Ezio DiBelardino
$75.00 to $135.00

Continental plus breakfast
6 rooms, 6 private baths
Children, over 12
No pets
Restricted smoking

In-town Georgian Revival mansion, circa 1899, meticulously restored in 1991, with luxury amenities and modern conveniences. Fabulous gourmet breakfasts served with freshly made espresso and capuccino. Walking distance to cultural attractions, downtown financial district and the local medical center. AAA 3-Diamonds.

HAM BISCUITS

2 cups flour
4 teaspoons baking powder
3/4 cup ground Smithfield ham
Pinch of salt
2 tablespoons shortening
3/4 cup milk

Sift flour and baking powder. Mix with ham and salt. Cut in shortening with knife until mixture has the consistency of meal. Add milk, handling as little as possible. Pat out with hands or roll on floured board. Cut out biscuits and bake in hot oven until brown. Makes 24 biscuits.

Submitted by:

Isle of Wight Inn
1607 S. Church Street
Smithfield, VA 23430
(804) 357-3176
Bob & Sylvia Hart,
Joan & Sam Earl
$49.00 to $99.00

Continental plus breakfast
10 rooms, 10 private baths
Children allowed
No pets
Restricted smoking
Mastercard, Visa, Am Ex, Discover

Luxurious bed & breakfast inn, with several very large suites with fireplaces and jacuzzis. Each room has air-conditioning, cable TV and telephone.

HAM ROLLS

1 lb. tub of margarine
2 - 3 teaspoons poppy seed
1 - 2 teaspoons dijon mustard
2 teaspoons Worcestershire sauce
2 teaspoons dehydrated onion
20 Pepperidge Farm party rolls (1 pack)
Sliced Swiss cheese
Sliced Virginia baked ham

Mix margarine with poppy seed, mustard, Worcestershire sauce and onion for spread. It should be made at least the night before serving. Spread will last several days. Take rolls and slice in half. Spread butter mixture on both sides of rolls. Put one slice each of ham and cheese on rolls. Fold rolls back over and keep in pan. Wrap pan in foil and bake at 300° for 30 minutes. Serve warm. Makes 5 servings.

Submitted by:

Applewood Colonial B&B
605 Richmond Rd.
Williamsburg, VA 23185
(800) 899-2753
Fred Strout
$65.00 to $100.00

Continental plus breakfast
4 rooms, 4 private baths
Children allowed
No pets
No smoking
Mastercard & Visa

Flemish-bond brick home built during the restoration of colonial Williamsburg. Parlor is decorated in a colonial style, featuring dentil crown molding. Crystal chandelier above dining room table. Suite has private entrance, fireplace and queen canopy bed.

OATMEAL SCONES

1 cup flour
1 teaspoon baking powder
1/2 teaspoon baking soda
1/4 teaspoon salt
1/4 cup sugar

1 stick butter
1 cup oats
1/2 cup raisins or currants
1/3 cup buttermilk
Melted butter

In food processor, or in medium bowl with pastry cutter or 2 knives, mix the first six ingredients. Stir in oats and raisins. Add buttermilk, mix until moist. Turn out on floured board and knead 7 - 8 times. Roll and pat to a 7" circle and cut into 8 equal wedges. Transfer to <u>ungreased</u> cookie sheet. Brush with melted butter and bake 15 minutes at 375°. Oatmeal scones are good for breakfast or can be served at tea time. Makes 8 scones.

Submitted by:

Old Slave Quarters
Reservations through Guesthouses B&B
P.O. Box 5737
Charlottesville, VA 22905
(804) 979-7264
Mary Hill Caperton
$80.00 to $100.00

Full breakfast
1 suite, with private bath
Children, over 6
No pets
Restricted smoking
Mastercard, Visa, Am Ex

Built 1814 - 1820, a most fascinating place to stay for interesting decor. Private entrance. Furnished with antiques and art objects. Sitting room with fireplace, two bedrooms, and couch which opens to double bed. Adjacent to University of VA and Fraternity Row, we are especially convenient for University guests.

SPICY CHEESE ROUNDS

3 cups grated sharp Cheddar cheese
1 cup freshly grated Parmesan cheese
3 tablespoons dried chives
3/4 - 1 teaspoon hot red pepper flakes
1/2 teaspoon fresh ground pepper
1 1/2 cups all-purpose flour
6 tablespoons cold, unsalted butter, in pieces
1 teaspoon salt
3/4 cup buttermilk

In large bowl toss together cheeses, chives and peppers. In food processor, mix flour, butter and salt. Pulse to mix, then toss with cheese mixture. Stir in buttermilk with a fork, just until it makes a ball. Knead on floured surface 10 - 15 seconds. Divide in half and roll into log 1" in diameter. Wrap in plastic and refrigerate until firm. Slice 1/8" thick and bake 1/2" apart at 325° for 30 minutes. If using 2 sheets, reverse after 15 minutes. Cool on a wire rack. Dough can be frozen in logs, ready to thaw, slice and bake. Baked wafers may be kept about a week in airtight tins.

Submitted by:

Cabin on the River
146 Crestview Dr.
Abingdon, VA 24210
(703) 628-8433
Sam & Janet Woolwine
$100.00/night to $500.00 wk.

Continental plus breakfast
2 rooms, 2 private baths
Children allowed
Pets allowed
Restricted smoking
Mastercard & Visa

We offer fishing and hiking and winter, corporate, or weekly rates. Absolute privacy for relaxing and reaquainting. Full access to kitchen with microwave, dishwasher and coffee maker. Gas grill on patio.

TROPICAL COFFEE CAKE

1/2 cup chopped pecans
1/2 cup flaked coconut
1/4 cup sugar
2 teaspoons grated orange rind
1 teaspoon ground cinnamon
1/2 cup butter or margarine, softened
1 cup sugar
2 eggs
8 oz. carton sour cream
1 teaspoon vanilla extract
2 cups all-purpose flour
1 teaspoon baking soda
1 teaspoon baking powder
Dash of salt

Combine first 5 ingredients in a bowl, set aside. Cream butter, gradually add 1 cup sugar, beating at medium speed of electric mixer. Add eggs, one at a time, beating after each addition. Add sour cream and vanilla. Combine flour and next 3 ingredients, add to creamed mixture. Beat well. Spoon half of batter into greased 9" square pan, sprinkle with half of pecan mixture. Repeat procedure with batter and pecan mixture. Gently swirl with a knife to create a marbled effect. Bake at 350° for 35 minutes or until a tester inserted in center comes out clean. Makes 9 - 12 servings.

Submitted by:

Fassifern B&B
RR# 5, Box 87
Lexington, VA 24450
(703) 463-1013
Frances Smith
$74.00 to $82.00

Continental plus breakfast
Five rooms, 5 private baths
No pets
Restricted smoking

Country brick manor home, circa 1867, situated on 3 1/2 tranquil acres. Just 2 miles north of historic Lexington in the Shenandoah Valley of VA. Adjacent to VA Horse Center. Easy access to I-64/I-81 on Route 39 West.

WALNUT-DATE PUFFS

Pastry:
8 oz. cream cheese, softened
1/2 lb. sweet butter, softened
2 cups sifted flour

Date Filling:
2 lbs. chopped, pitted dates
1 cup chopped walnuts
1 cup brown sugar
1 cup water

Soften cream cheese and butter to room temperature. Mix in flour, knead and form into ball. Refrigerate overnight. Remove from refrigerator and soften for 3 hours. Roll out thin (1/8" - 1/4") and cut into 3" squares. Put one tablespoon of filling in the middle of each square. Pinch the two opposite corners together. Bake at 375° for 12 - 15 minutes. Sift powdered sugar over the top while warm. These freeze well and can defrost quickly for tea. Makes 3 dozen puffs.

Submitted by:

The Claiborne House
119 Claiborne Ave.
Rocky Mount, VA 24151
(703) 483-4616
Margaret & Jim Young
$65.00 to $115.00

Full breakfast
5 rooms, 5 private baths
Children allowed
No pets
Restricted smoking
Mastercard & Visa

Elegant Victorian surrounded by charming English gardens. Walnut paneled ceilings and 130 foot wraparound porch. Awaken in luxurious antique appointed suites with hot coffee outside the door. Romantic candlelight gourmet breakfast.

MISCELLANEOUS FARE

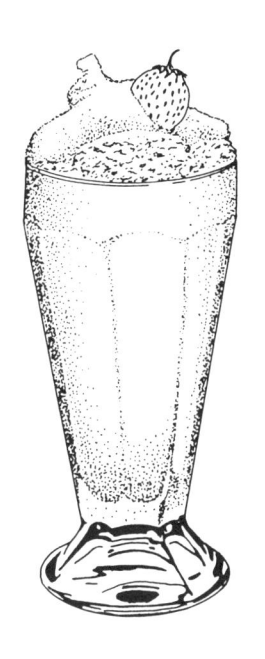

BAKED EGG IN TOMATO

4 large, ripe tomatoes
1/4 cup grated sharp Cheddar cheese
1/4 cup fresh, soft grated bread crumbs
1 tablespoon minced parsley
1/4 teaspoon salt
1/8 teaspoon pepper
4 large, fresh country eggs
2 tablespoons melted butter

Preheat oven to 425°. Slice top off of each tomato and scoop out pulp. Place in greased pie pan and bake 5 - 7 minutes. Mix cheese, bread crumbs, parsley, salt and pepper together. Break eggs, one at a time, and slide one into each tomato. Add approximately 2 tablespoons of bread/cheese mixture to each tomato and drizzle with melted butter. Bake 15 to 20 minutes until eggs are just set. Garnish with sprig of basil. Serve immediately. Makes 4 servings.

Submitted by:

The Holladay House
155 West Main Street
Orange, VA 22960
(703) 672-4893
Pete and Phebe Holladay
$75.00 to $185.00

Full breakfast
6 rooms, 5 private baths
Children allowed
No pets
Restricted smoking
Mastercard & Visa

A restored Federal-style home, circa 1830, in the Holladay family since 1899. The large comfortable rooms are furnished with family pieces and each room features its own sitting area. Breakfast is normally served in guests' own rooms.

COUNTRY BAKED APPLES

3 lbs. peeled, sliced apples
1/4 cup sugar
1 teaspoon cinnamon
1/2 stick butter or margarine

Peel and slice apples. Put in baking dish, cover with sugar and sprinkle with cinnamon. Put pats of butter or margarine on top. Bake at 350°, or microwave for 20 - 25 minutes. Makes 8 servings.

Submitted by:

Norfields Farm B&B
Route 1, Box 477
Gordonsville, VA 22942
(703) 832-2952
Teresa Norton
$50.00 to $75.00

Full breakfast
4 rooms, 2 private baths
Children allowed
Pets allowed
No smoking

500 acres at the Blue Ridge Foothills. A working dairy farm, fourth generation. Old farmhouse, circa 1850, is filled with antiques and family treasures. Seclusion, country charm, and warm hospitality make us special. Monticello & Montpelier 30 minutes away. 45 minutes from Skyline Drive.

HOT SPICED FRUIT

1 can pear halves
1 can apricot halves
1 can light sweet cherries
1 can pineapple chunks
Juice of 1 lemon
1/4 cup packed brown sugar

1/4 teaspoon nutmeg
1/4 teaspoon cinnamon
1/8 teaspoon ground cloves
2 tablespoons butter or margarine

Sour cream for topping

Drain fruits, reserving 3/4 cup of combined juices. Arrange fruit in 2 quart casserole, sprinkle with lemon juice. Combine 3/4 cup reserved juice with brown sugar, nutmeg, cinnamon and cloves. Pour over fruit. Dot with butter. Bake at 350° for 20 minutes. Serve topped with sour cream, and sprinkled with nutmeg. Makes 8 - 10 servings.

Submitted by:

Heritage House, Inc.
Main and Piedmont Streets
Washington, VA 22747
(703) 675-3207
Jean & Frank Scott
$95.00 to $125.00 (suite)

Full breakfast
4 rooms, 4 private baths
No children
No pets
No smoking
Mastercard & Visa

1837 manor house in "Little" Washington, VA, a village surveyed by young George Washington. Used as a Civil War headquarters. Heirloom antiques, international collectibles, gourmet breakfasts and gorgeous Blue Ridge views. Central to fine dining, antiquing, hiking, and nature. Relaxed, comfortable, pretty!

KRINGLE FRUIT WRAP

2 cups flour
1 cup sour cream
2 sticks butter or margarine (room temp.)
Canned fruit
Chopped nuts
Raisins

Icing:
3/4 box confectioners sugar
2 tablespoons melted margarine
2 teaspoons vanilla

Mix flour, sour cream, and butter together until soft. Refrigerate overnight. This mixture can be kept longer, but cover tightly. Next day, roll dough into a rectangle. Fill with canned fruit, nuts, raisins, or your choice of fillings. Fold over at center and ends, crimping closed. Bake for 20 minutes in 350° oven. Ice. Makes 12 servings.

Submitted by:

Sleepy Hollow Farm B&B
16280 Blue Ridge Turnpike
Gordonsville, VA 22942
(703) 832-5555
Beverley Allison,
Dorsey Comer
$60.00 to $125.00

Full breakfast
7 rooms
Children allowed
Ask about permission for pets
Smoking allowed
Mastercard & Visa

Enjoy country life in charming old farmhouse or the chestnut cottage. On an historic road, rolling through lush, beautiful VA countryside. In the heart of horse, cattle and sheep farms. Children's play area, horseback riding, golf available. Home-grown herbs and flowers.

ORANGE FRUIT SOUP

2 tablespoons quick tapioca
1 1/2 cups water
1 tablespoon sugar
Dash of salt
1/2 cup frozen concentrated orange juice
1/2 cup diced orange sections
1 medium banana, sliced
5 - 6 fresh strawberries, sliced
Garnish:
Whole strawberries

Combine tapioca and water in saucepan. Cook and stir over medium heat until mixture comes to a boil. Remove from heat. Add sugar, salt and concentrated orange juice and stir to blend. Cool. Stir after 15 minutes, cover and chill. Before serving fold in oranges, bananas and strawberries. Reserve some whole strawberries for garnish. Makes 5 - 6 servings.

Submitted by:

Oak Spring Farm & Vineyard
Route 1, Box 356
Raphine, VA 24472
 (Lexington area)
(703) 377-2398
Pat & Jim Tichenor
$45.00 to $65.00

Continental plus breakfast
3 rooms, 3 private baths
Children, over 16
No pets
No smoking
Mastercard & Visa

Recently restored circa 1826 plantation house featuring modern conveniences, period antiques, family and other accessories collected during world-wide military travels. 40 acre farm & vineyard affords warm hospitality in a picturesque setting in a quiet rural area.

STAR ANISE SPICED APPLES WITH CUSTARD YOGURT

2 cups whole fresh cranberries
5 large Golden Delicious apples, peeled, cored, cut into eighths
1 - 2" cinnamon stick
2 teaspoons whole cloves
1 teaspoon star anise
3 cups apple juice or white grape juice
1/2 cup sugar
2 - 6 oz. containers vanilla yogurt (custard style)

Preheat oven to 350°. Wash and pick over cranberries. Place in 9" x 13" x 2" Pyrex baking dish. Peel, core and eighth the apples. Spread apples on top of cranberries, placing cinnamon stick in the center. Sprinkle cloves and star anise on top of apples. Pour juice over apples. Sprinkle with sugar. Cover with aluminum foil. Bake for 50 - 60 minutes. Check for doneness. Apples should be tender (soft), but should still hold their shape. Allow to cool, then remove spices. Serve in individual bowls or goblets with a dollop of yogurt. Makes 8 servings.

Submitted by:

Ashton Country House
1205 Middlebrook Road
Staunton, VA 24401
(703) 885-7819
Sheila Kennedy &
Stanley Polanski
$65.00 to $80.00

Full breakfast
4 rooms, 4 private baths
Children, over 16
No pets
No smoking

Greek Revival brick home, circa 1860, on 20 peaceful acres at the outskirts of Staunton. Guest rooms are comfortably furnished with queen-size or double bed. Breakfast and afternoon tea are prepared by a professionally trained chef, and often accompanied by live piano music. Historic attractions and fine dining are nearby.

UNCLE ED'S WAKE-UP CALL

1 large, very ripe banana
2 tablespoons crushed pineapple
3 ripe or frozen strawberries
4 packets Equal sugar substitute
45 ounces orange juice

Place banana, pineapple, strawberries and sugar substitute into blender. Add half of orange juice. Blend at highest speed for two minutes. Pour remaining orange juice through the center. Best served immediately, but may be chilled and reblended immediately before serving. Makes 6 servings.

Submitted by:

House of Laird
335 South Main St.
Chatham, VA 24531
(804) 432-2523
Mr. & Mrs. Ed (Cecil) Laird
$38.00 to $57.00

Full breakfast
3 rooms, 3 private baths
Children, over 12
No pets
Restricted smoking
Mastercard & Visa

Affordable, luxurious getaways. Century-old Greek Revival lovingly restored and professionally decorated. Oriental rugs, antiques, imported moldings, wall coverings and fabrics, canopied beds and fireplaces. Antique china and period silver. Tea. Small, historic inn where guests receive gracious, southern hospitality.

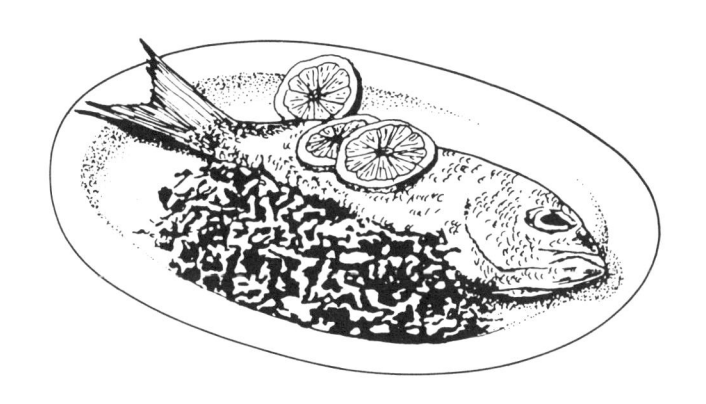

NOT JUST
FOR
BREAKFAST...

BROCCOLI CRUNCH

1 cup broccoli flowerettes (3 - 4 stalks)
1/2 cup raisins
1/2 cup chopped walnuts
1/2 cup chopped red onion
1 cup light mayonnaise
1/4 cup sugar (or less to taste)
3 teaspoons white vinegar
10 pieces crisp bacon (microwaved)
1/2 cup red grapes

Mix together broccoli flowerettes, raisins, chopped walnuts and red onion. Combine mayonnaise, sugar and vinegar. Crumble bacon and mix with mayonnaise mixture. Pour over the broccoli. Make a decorative "X" on top with the red grapes. Looks great!!! Makes 6 servings.

Submitted by:

The Widow Kip's
Route 1, Box 117
Mt. Jackson, VA 22842
(703) 477-2400
Betty Luse
$65.00 to $85.00

Full breakfast
7 rooms, 7 private baths
Children allowed
Pets allowed
Smoking allowed
Mastercard & Visa

1830 Colonial farmhouse on 7 acres of meadows and pastureland. Two restored cottages, (originally a hen house and washhouse) flank the inn, creating a courtyard. Canopied beds, fireplaces, and sleigh beds covered with old-fashioned quilts. 32' pool on premises.

BRUNSWICK STEW

3 1/2 lbs. chicken breasts & thighs
Salt & pepper to taste
1/3 cup vegetable oil
1 large onion, chopped
1 cup celery, chopped
1 - 16 oz. can stewed tomatoes
1/2 teaspoon dried basil
2 cups frozen lima beans
2 cups frozen niblets corn
2 tablespoons Worcestershire sauce
1/8 teaspoon hot sauce
1 - 2 tablespoons butter

Season chicken pieces with salt and pepper, and fry in vegetable oil in large kettle until browned on all sides. Remove chicken with tongs. Add celery and onion to drippings. Sauté until onion is tender. Return chicken to kettle, and add tomatoes, basil, and water as necessary to keep from sticking to pan. Cook slowly, covered, until chicken is tender, about 35 minutes. Remove from heat, take out chicken pieces and remove meat from bone. Cut meat into bite-sized pieces and return to kettle (discarding bones and skin). Add lima beans, corn, Worcestershire, and hot sauce. Cook over low heat until vegetables are just tender. Stir in butter. Can be served at once, but it is best refrigerated and reheated slowly, for serving the next day. This is an updated version of an authentic Colonial Virginia recipe, and a great make-ahead dish! Serves 6.

Submitted by:

The Inn at Narrow Passage
U.S. 11 S. (I-81, Exit 283)
Woodstock, VA 22664
(703) 459-8000
Ellen & Ed Markel
$55.00 to $90.00

Full breakfast
12 rooms, 10 private baths
Children allowed
No pets
Restricted smoking
Mastercard & Visa

This historic Shenandoah Valley inn has been serving travelers for over 250 years. Recent additions provide comfortable guest rooms, a lovely colonial dining room for breakfast by the fire, and executive conference facilities. Country setting with 5 acres, great for fishing & hiking. Near caverns, vineyards, Civil War battlefields & restaurants.

CHANGUA POTATOES

2 tablespoons olive oil
3/4 cup milk
1 whole scallion, bearded
2 scallions, chopped
5 cups boiling potatoes, in matchstick julienne

1/4 cup sun-dried tomatoes, snipped
Salt to taste
Freshly ground pepper to taste
Fresh cilantro to taste, chopped

In nonstick, 10" - 12" frying pan, place 1 tablespoon of oil, the milk, 1 whole scallion, the potatoes, tomatoes, salt and pepper. Cover and cook a few minutes until the milk boils up through all the potatoes. Remove lid and continue cooking, shaking periodically, until all liquid is evaporated. Remove the scallion if you like. Stir the potatoes around, loosening them from the pan. Drizzle the remaining oil around the sides of the pan. Increase the heat slightly and continue cooking. Shake the potatoes or slide a spatula around the edges to keep them loose in the pan. When the edges begin to brown, sprinkle the top with the 2 chopped scallions, and a little of the chopped cilantro. Turn the potatoes over either by flipping, or inverting the pan on a plate, then sliding back into the pan. Cook for a few more minutes before sliding onto a serving plate or cutting board. Cut into wedges. Garnish with chopped cilantro on the potatoes, as well as leafy sprigs on the side. Makes 4 - 6 servings.

Submitted by:

Langhorne Manor
313 Washington St.
Lynchburg, VA 24504
(804) 846-4667
Jaime & Jaynee Acevedo
$70.00 to $95.00

Full breakfast
4 rooms, 4 private baths
No pets
No smoking
Mastercard, Visa, Am Ex

On historic Diamond Hill, 27 room antebellum mansion filled with warmth, antiques & family heirlooms. High ceilings, spacious rooms, and central a/c. Art gallery, architecturally magnificent neighborhood & lavish creative breakfasts. Watch our renovation or enjoy area history and attractions. Business rates, special weekends.

CHICKEN AMANDINE

- 1 - 20 oz. can pineapple slices in juice
- 4 boneless, skinless chicken breast halves
- 1 teaspoon vegetable oil
- 1 cup sliced mushrooms
- 1/2 teaspoon tarragon, crumbled
- 2 tablespoons sliced almonds
- 1/2 teaspoon margarine
- 1/2 cup chopped parsley
- 1 tablespoon dijon mustard
- 1 tablespoon grated lemon peel
- 1 1/2 teaspoons cornstarch

Drain pineapple, reserving juice. Pound chicken breasts to flatten. Heat oil in non-stick skillet. Add chicken and sauté 4 - 5 minutes on each side, adding mushrooms and tarragon before turning chicken. Remove chicken and mushrooms to serving dish and keep warm. Sauté pineapple slices in same skillet. Remove to dish with chicken. Sauté almonds in margarine until golden brown. Stir in parsley. Combine reserved pineapple juice, mustard, lemon peel, and cornstarch. Add to skillet. Cook, stirring, until sauce boils and thickens. Spoon over chicken and pineapple. Very good! Makes 4 servings.

Submitted by:

King's Victorian Inn
Route 2, Box 622
Hot Springs, VA 24445
(703) 839-3134
Liz & Richard King
$75.00 to $85.00

Full breakfast
5 rooms, 3 private baths
No children
No pets
Restricted smoking

High Victorian house, circa 1899, with antiques, stained glass windows, skylight, turrets, bay windows, and a verandah which extends around most of the house. Our stair has several landings and runs in several different directions. Nestled in a grove of beautiful old maple trees, 150 yards from Homestead 5-star resort.

CHICKEN DIVAN

6 chicken breasts
Water to cover chicken
Salt to taste
Pepper to taste
1 slice onion
2 pkgs. frozen broccoli spears

2 cups cream of chicken soup
1 cup mayonnaise
1 tablespoon lemon juice
1/2 teaspoon curry powder
1/4 cup diced cheese
1/4 cup bread crumbs

Place chicken breasts in water with salt, pepper and onion. Cook until tender. Drain, cool, debone and skin. Cook broccoli by package directions (or use fresh broccoli). Drain broccoli and place in bottom of casserole dish. Arrange chicken breasts on top. Make a sauce with the soup, mayonnaise, lemon juice and curry powder. Spoon over chicken and broccoli. Top with the cheese and bread crumbs. Bake at 400° until bubbly and browned on top. Makes 6 servings.

Submitted by:

Burger's Country Inn
Route 2, Box 564
Natural Bridge, VA 24578
(703) 291-2464
Frances B. Burger
$35.00 to $50.00

Continental plus breakfast
4 rooms, 2 private baths
Children allowed
Pets allowed
Restricted smoking

Historic inn furnished in antiques and country collectibles. Quiet, comfortable, relaxing, friendly atmosphere. Large porches, deck and yard adjoining woods. Croquet & hiking available with golf and horseback riding nearby. 13 miles from historic Lexington and 1 mile from Natural Bridge Resort. Real Southern hospitality.

CHICKEN GRAPE SALAD

1/2 cup nonfat yogurt
2 teaspoons mayonnaise
1 teaspoon dijon mustard
Herbs or light spices to taste
2 chicken breasts, cooked & cubed
3 scallions, sliced small
15 green, sweet grapes, halved

Mix yogurt, mayonnaise, mustard, and any herbs or light spices. Toss chicken in mixture. Add scallions and grapes. Serve with French bread and sorbet for dessert. Makes 2 servings.

Submitted by:

Lynchburg Mansion Inn
  Bed & Breakfast
405 Madison Street
Lynchburg, VA 24504
(800) 352-1199
Bob & Mauranna Sherman
$84.00 to $129.00

Full breakfast
4 rooms (includes suites),
  4 private baths
Children allowed
No pets
No smoking
Mastercard, Visa, Am Ex

Private 9,000 square foot mansion, on 1/2 acre in Garden Hill Historic District. Our street is still paved in turn-of-the-century brick. Relax in Laura Ashley Country French Room, mahogany furnishings in English Room, or shells & wicker of our Nantucket. Nightly turn-down service, morning newspaper, TV, HBO, and padded satin hangers.

CHICKEN POT PIE WITH BUTTERMILK BISCUITS

6 tablespoons butter
6 tablespoons flour
2 cups chicken broth
1 cup milk or half & half
1/2 teaspoon white pepper

1 cup frozen baby peas
1 cup mushrooms, sautéed in butter
4 cups cooked chicken, cut into pieces

Buttermilk Biscuits:
2 cups self-rising flour
1/2 teaspoon baking soda

1/3 cup vegetable oil
2/3 cup buttermilk

Make a cream sauce from the first five ingredients, correct the seasoning; add peas and mushrooms. Put chicken in a greased casserole dish. Pour cream sauce over chicken. For biscuits: Combine all ingredients, turn out on floured board. Roll out dough, fold over once, cut biscuits. Place biscuits on top of casserole. Bake at 450° for 10 - 15 minutes. Good served with tossed green salad, glazed carrots. Serves 4.

Submitted by:

Edgewood Farm B&B
RR # 2, Box 303
Stanardsville, VA 22973
(804) 985-3782
Norman & Eleanor Schwartz
$50.00 to $65.00

Full breakfast
3 rooms, 2 private baths
Children allowed
No pets
Restricted smoking
Mastercard & Visa

Colonial Virginia farmhouse on a 130 acre farm in the foothills of the Blue Ridge Mountains. Originally built in 1790, the house has been faithfully restored and decorated with antiques and period furniture. Relax in the country and visit our herb and perennial nursery.

COLONIAL OYSTER STEW

1 sheet frozen puff
  pastry
1 egg
2 cups heavy cream
16 oz. oysters, selects
Salt and white pepper
  to taste

1 teaspoon Old Bay
  seafood seasoning
8 oz. Surry bacon,
  diced and cooked
1 bunch chives,
  snipped and minced

Preheat oven to 375°. Cut puff pastry sheet into desired shape using cookie cutter. Beat egg. Place pastry onto cookie sheet lined with parchment paper. Brush beaten egg lightly onto pastry. Bake pastry 15 - 20 minutes or until golden brown. Remove from oven and cool 15 minutes. Cut pastry in half horizontally. Place bottom halves into 4 separate soup bowls. Reserve tops. Heat cream in large sauté pan to boiling. Simmer cream and reduce to half. Add oysters, salt, pepper, and Old Bay seasoning. Cook oysters until edges start to curl, about 3 minutes. Add cooked bacon and chives. Cook 30 seconds. Divide mixture into prepared soup bowls. Place puff pastry tops on each one. Serve immediately. (Can be served at breakfast.) Makes 4 servings.

Submitted by:

Williamsburg Sampler B&B
922 Jamestown Road
Williamsburg, VA 23185
(800) 722-1169
(804) 253-0398
Helen & Ike Sisane
$85.00 to $90.00

Full breakfast
4 rooms, 4 private baths
Children, over 12
No pets
No smoking

Elegant 18th century plantation style brick colonial features famous "Skip Lunch" Breakfast. Romantic guest rooms with four-poster beds and reproductions assures quiet, restful slumber. Antiques, pewter, samplers; walking distance to historic Colonial Williamsburg. Awarded AAA 3-Diamonds.

DINNER-IN-A-DISH

1 lb. ground beef
1/2 cup sliced green onions
3/4 cup milk
8 oz. pkg. cream cheese, softened
3 cups whole kernel corn (drained) or frozen cooked corn
Dash of pepper

3 cups noodles (6 oz.), cooked & drained
1 can cream of mushroom soup
1/4 cup chopped pimiento or mild sweet red pepper (opt.)
1 - 1 1/2 teaspoons salt

Brown meat. Drain off fat. Add onion. Stir in milk and cream cheese until well-blended. Add remaining ingredients. Pour into 2 quart casserole. Bake at 350° for 30 minutes. Needs only a tossed green salad, rolls, and a fruit cup to round out the meal. Makes 6 - 8 servings.

Submitted by:

Memory House
6404 N. Washington Blvd.
Arlington, VA 22205
(703) 534-4607
John & Marlys McGrath
$65.00 to $70.00

Continental plus breakfast
2 rooms, 1 private bath
Children, over 12, and infants in cribs
No pets
No smoking

Ornate, artistically restored Victorian, old-fashioned comfort, friendship, and charm. Period antiques, prize-winning handicrafts, and collectibles. 1 block to subway, 3 blocks from I-66 via exit 69, 10 minutes to monument area of Washington, D.C. Ideal location for exploring by subway or car. Traditional lifestyles only, please.

FRESH VEGETABLE PIZZA

2 cans Pillsbury crescent rolls
1/2 cup mayonnaise
8 oz. cream cheese, softened
1/2 pkg. Hidden Valley Ranch dressing mix
Freshly grated Cheddar cheese

Finely chopped vegetables of your choice: (Select a few or all)
Green pepper, onion, broccoli, carrots, cauliflower, seeded tomatoes, mushrooms, black olives, zucchini, cucumber, etc.

Flour surface. Roll out rolls very flat. Bake at 350° for 5 - 10 minutes until brown. Mix mayonnaise, softened cream cheese and dressing mix. Spread on cooled dough. Top with finely chopped vegetables, ending with grated cheese. Cut into squares. Use waxed paper between layers. Chill for several hours before serving. Makes 60 squares.

Submitted by:

Chester House
43 Chester Street
Front Royal, VA 22630
(703) 635-3937
Bill & Ann Wilson
$55.00 to $150.00

Continental plus breakfast
7 rooms, 3 private baths
Children, over 12
No pets
Restricted smoking
Mastercard, Visa, Am Ex

Stately Georgian mansion with extensive formal gardens in Historic District. Quiet, relaxed atmosphere in elegant surroundings, an "oasis" in the heart of town. Walking distance to antique & gift shops & historic attractions. Short drive to Skyline Caverns, Shenandoah River, golf, tennis, hiking, skiing, horseback riding, and restaurants.

GOVERNOR'S TRACE PEANUT SOUP

1 can Campbell's celery soup
1 can milk
1 chicken bouillon cube
1 cup water
1/2 cup crunchy peanut butter
1 small loaf French bread
Unsalted peanuts

Combine first four ingredients in pan over medium heat. Do not boil. Add peanut butter and stir until melted through. If not thick enough, add more peanut butter by tablespoonful until desired consistency. Cut French bread loaf into sixteenths, leaving some crust on each piece. Toast until crisp in toaster oven for Colonial bread dippers known as "sippets". You can also use smooth peanut butter and garnish with chopped unsalted peanuts. Makes a wonderful winter's night main course dinner for two, or first course for four. Yield: 2 or 4 servings.

Submitted by:

Governor's Trace
  Bed & Breakfast
303 Capitol Landing Road
Williamsburg, VA 23185
(804) 229-7552
Sue & Dick Lake
$85.00 to $115.00

Continental plus
2 rooms, 2 private baths
No children
No pets
No smoking
Mastercard & Visa

Rekindle romance in the closest B&B to Colonial Williamsburg. Lovely old Georgian brick lets you step into history just one door away. Candlelit, antique-furnished, spacious rooms offer choice of tall, four-poster bed, kingsize bed with working fireplace in room, or full Colonial style canopy bed with private screened porch.

HEARTY FISH CHOWDER

2 1/2 lbs. potatoes, peeled, and sliced 1/8" thick
2 large yellow onions, halved and sliced
Water to cover potatoes and onions
1/2 teaspoon pepper
1 teaspoon salt
2 tablespoons butter or margarine
1 - 12 oz. can evaporated milk
1/2 lb. "sea legs", sliced
1/2 lb. white fish
1 tablespoon butter or margarine
1 teaspoon lemon juice
1 - 6 oz. can small shrimp
1/4 cup chopped fresh parsley

Put potatoes and onions in large heavy pot with just enough water to cover. Add pepper, salt and 2 tablespoons butter. Cover pot. Simmer until potatoes are tender. Add evaporated milk, stir, cover, and turn off heat. Poach "sea legs" and fish in small pan with 1 tablespoon butter and lemon juice. Add to potatoes with shrimp, stir, bring to simmer, and add parsley. Adjust seasoning. Chowder improves with "sitting time." We prepare it early to serve in the evening. Serve with hot French bread and salad. Makes 4 large bowls with leftovers.

Submitted by:

Seward House Inn
Route 10, P.O. Box 352
Surry, VA 23883
(804) 294-3810
Jacqueline Bayer & Cynthia Erskine
$65.00 to $95.00

Full breakfast
4 rooms, 2 private baths
Children allowed
No pets
Restricted smoking
Am Ex

Restored 1900 country home built by Jacqueline Bayer's great uncle and aunt. Dr. Seward was a physician. Small guest cottage was his treatment room and pharmacy. Furnished with furniture and photographs from both innkeepers' families. We bake our own bread, can & freeze our garden produce & grow herbs for our meals.

JAMBALAYA HAM SOUP

1 - 1 1/4 to 1 1/2 lb. meaty ham bone
1 sliced onion
1 cup celery leaves
2 - 3 parsley sprigs
1/4 teaspoon ground red pepper
5 cups water
1/4 teaspoon black pepper
1 cup chopped celery
1/2 cup chopped onion
1 small clove garlic, minced
2 tablespoons butter
8 oz. tomato sauce
1/4 cup catsup
1/4 cup long grain rice
10 oz. pkg. frozen cut okra
1 - 4 1/2 oz. can shrimp, drained

Combine ham bone, onion, celery leaves, parsley sprigs, red pepper, water and black pepper. Bring to boiling; reduce heat. Cover and simmer 30 - 45 minutes. Remove bone. Cool and cut off meat, chop. Discard bone, strain broth. Cook chopped celery, onion and garlic in butter until tender. Stir in broth, ham, tomato sauce, catsup and uncooked rice. Bring to boiling, reduce heat. Cover and simmer 15 minutes. Add okra and drained shrimp. Return to boiling. Reduce heat. Cover and simmer 5 minutes more. Makes 6 servings.

Submitted by:

The William Catlin House
2304 E. Broad Street
Richmond, VA 23223
(804) 780-3746
Robert & Josie Martin
$70.00 to $140.00

Full breakfast
5 rooms, 3 private baths
Children, over 10
No pets
Restricted smoking
Mastercard & Visa

Richmond's first and oldest B&B. 1845 restored home decorated entirely with antiques, reproductions, canopy & poster beds, Oriental rugs, and crystal chandeliers. Central air-conditioning, fireplaces, and lots of Southern hospitality. Room rates include all taxes.

LITHUANIAN COLD BEET SOUP

1 can whole beets (or fresh, young, cooked beets, with the greens)
2 cucumbers
1 bunch scallions
Fresh dill to taste
1 quart buttermilk
1 cup sour cream
1 hard-boiled egg, chopped, for garnish

Drain beets, reserve liquid. Grate beets coarsely and add to the liquid. Peel and chop cucumbers, scallions and dill. Add to the beets. Mix with buttermilk and sour cream. Garnish with chopped hard-boiled egg. Serve with boiled young potatoes sprinkled with dill.

Submitted by:

Upper Byrd Farm B&B
6452 River Road West
Columbia, VA 23038
(804) 842-2240
Ivona Kaz-Jepsen &
Maya Laurinaitis
$60.00 to $70.00

Full breakfast
4 rooms, 2 semi-private baths
Children, over 12
No pets
Restricted smoking

Turn-of-the-century farmhouse nestled in the Virginia countryside on 26 acres, overlooking the James River. Visit Ashlawn and Monticello. See the State's capitol, or simply relax by the fire, surrounded by antiques and original art.

PORK CHOPS WITH APPLES & SAUERKRAUT

4 pork chops, trimmed, cut 1/2" thick
Vegetable oil for browning
1 medium onion, sliced & separated into rings
1/8 teaspoon instant garlic flakes
3 cups sauerkraut, drained
3/4 cup apple juice
1 1/2 teaspoons caraway seed
1/4 teaspoon salt
1/4 teaspoon thyme
1/4 teaspoon pepper
1 cup red cooking apple slices, cored, but unpeeled

Brown chops in oil in nonstick pan and set aside. (Can omit this step if necessary). Place half of all ingredients except pork chops and apples into bottom of slow cooker (crock pot). Add the pork chops. Place the remaining half of ingredients on top. Top with apple slices. Cover slow cooker, and cook on slow for 6 - 8 hours, or on high for 4 hours. Makes 4 servings.

Submitted by:

Upland Manor
Route 1, Box 375
Nellysford, VA 22958
(804) 361-1101
Stan & Karen Pugh
$85.00 to $115.00

Continental plus breakfast
10 rooms, 10 private baths
Children, over 12
No pets
No smoking
Mastercard & Visa

Restored 1880 manor house offers romantic, luxurious rooms, some with whirlpool tubs. Antiquing, golfing, skiing, hot air ballooning, all outdoor sports, a nap in the backyard hammock, or rocking on the big front porch. 14 peaceful acres near Wintergreen Resort, between historic Charlottesville and the Blue Ridge Mountains.

SEAFOOD FETTUCINI

8 oz. pkg. fettucini
1/4 cup melted butter
1/2 cup fresh grated Parmesan cheese
1/2 cup half and half
1/8 teaspoon fresh black pepper
1/8 teaspoon cayenne pepper
1/2 carton sour cream
1/4 cup fresh chopped parsley
1 lb. fresh shrimp, peeled, deveined
1/2 lb. small, fresh sea scallops
Lemon butter

Prepare noodles as package directs, drain and keep warm. In flat skillet, combine butter, cheese, half and half, black pepper, cayenne pepper, and sour cream. Warm until cheese blends in with mixture. Add parsley. In another skillet, toss shrimp and scallops in lemon butter. Add to cheese mixture, and serve over noodles. 8 servings.

Submitted by:

Victoria & Albert Inn
  & Antiques
224 Oak Hill St.
Abingdon, VA 24210
(703) 676-2797
Frank & Lesley Hubbard
$75.00 to $85.00

Full breakfast
4 rooms, 2 private baths
Children, over 12
No pets
No smoking
Mastercard & Visa

Step back to a more gracious time and be pampered in Victorian style. Exquisite antique furnishings, gas log fireplaces, wicker ladened porches and superb "silver service" breakfast. Delightful walk to world renowned Barter Theatre & Olde Abingdon shopping.

"ST. MOOR" HOUSE HOME-GROWN SPEARMINT TEA

1 quart cold tap water
5 tea bags of your choice
1 cup sugar

5 stalks of well-leaved mint plants

Rinse teapot or pitcher with hot water. Place tea bags inside. Bring 1 quart cold tap water to a boil and pour over tea bags. Add mint plants which have been rinsed well under cold tap water. Let tea steep about 30 minutes, so total flavor is achieved (less than 30 minutes if you prefer less mint flavor). Serve in tall glasses stacked with ice. Garnish with mint cluster. Add cold water to weaken, as desired. Makes 8 - 10 servings.

Submitted by:

"St. Moor" House
Route 1, Box 136
Monroe, VA 24574
(804) 929-8228
Jean & John Camm
$46.00 to $59.00

Full breakfast
3 rooms, 2 private baths
Children allowed
No pets
Restricted smoking

Located in beautiful central VA, adjacent peach & apple orchards. House view of majestic High Peak Mtn., several hundred acres to stroll: woods, pastures, horses, cows, en route. Cathedral roof, massive fireplace, antiques, "olde" VA warm and gracious hospitality.

STUFFED BLACK SEA BASS VIRGINIA

1 - 3 lb. fish
1 cup Virginia blue crabmeat
1 cup Virginia sweet white corn (blanched)
Seasonings optional (salt, white pepper, parsley, etc.)
Chardonnay vine
Sauce:
1 cup of white sauce recipe (your choice)

Salt or 1 teaspoon Worcestershire sauce
3 tablespoons parsley
1 cup Eastern Shore oysters and juice (poached)
1/2 cup Surry County bacon
Fresh lemon juice (optional)

Vinegared field greens

Preheat oven to 325°. Leave skin of bass intact and clean. Scale and eviscerate fish. Stuff fish with Virginia blue crabmeat, Virginia sweet white corn (blanched), and seasonings optional. Bake in oven or smoke, using Chardonnay vines for approximately 40 minutes. Serve with oyster and bacon sauce. For sauce: Make 1 cup of white sauce recipe of your choice. Season sauce well with salt or Worcestershire sauce. Shortly before serving, bring sauce to a boil and add parsley, poached oysters and juice, bacon and lemon juice. Serve sea bass over vinegared field greens. Makes 4 servings.

Submitted by:

Mr. Patrick Henry's Inn
2300 East Broad Street
Richmond, VA 23223
(804) 644-1322
Jim & Lynn News
$95.00 to $135.00

Full breakfast
4 suites, 4 private baths
Children allowed
No pets
Smoking allowed
Mastercard, Visa, Am Ex

Pre-Civil War inn, on Historic Church Hill: gourmet restaurant, English pub, and garden patio. Each suite has fireplace and kitchenette, some private porches. Private parties, business functions, rehearsal dinners & wedding receptions. Lunch and dinner served Monday - Saturday. Reservations suggested.

TEA TIME TARTS

2 envelopes gelatin
1/2 cup cold water
3 cups cooked, sieved pumpkin
1 cup milk
1 1/2 cups honey

1 teaspoon salt
1 teaspoon nutmeg
1 teaspoon ginger
1 cup chopped pecans
12 baked tart shells

Soften gelatin in cold water. Combine all other ingredients, except nuts, and heat over boiling water. Add softened gelatin and stir until it is dissolved. Cool. Stir in nuts. Fill tart shells and chill until firm. A very nice treat for afternoon tea. Makes 12 tarts.

Submitted by:

The Madison House
  Bed & Breakfast
413 Madison Street
Lynchburg, VA 24504
(804) 528-1503
Irene & Dale Smith
$70.00 to $95.00

Full breakfast
4 rooms, 4 private baths
No children
No pets
Restricted smoking
Mastercard & Visa

Outstanding accommodations on "Quality Row", in the heart of the Garland Hill Historic District. Lynchburg's finest Victorian bed & breakfast. Large, comfortable bedchambers, antique-filled parlors, and afternoon tea.

TOMATO, GARLIC & PARMESAN SOUP

2 medium onions
2 shallots
12 cloves garlic, thinly sliced
2 leeks, white part only
3 tablespoons olive oil (extra virgin if possible)
8 ripe tomatoes (or whole Italian canned tomatoes)
1 - 1 1/2 cups chicken stock
1/2 cup heavy cream or half & half (optional)
Salt & freshly ground black pepper to taste
8 slices French bread
1 cup grated Parmesan or Romano cheese
8 large fresh basil leaves

Chop onions and shallots finely, clean leeks thoroughly, and slice crosswise thinly. Sauté onion, shallots and leeks in olive oil about 5 minutes, or until tender (not browned). Blanch ripe tomatoes a few seconds in boiling water, then peel, cut in half and squeeze out juice and seeds. Liquify tomato pulp in food processor or blender. Add liquified tomato to onion mixture, add garlic. Bring to a boil, add chicken stock and simmer for 15 - 20 minutes. Season with salt and pepper. Toast French bread slices and brush lightly with olive oil. Slice basil leaves thinly. Just before serving soup, add cream to taste (if desired), heat to simmering, just until heated through. Serve soup topped with 2 slices French bread sprinkled with Parmesan cheese. Garnish with basil leaves. Serve with extra Parmesan. 4 servings.

Submitted by:

The Garden and the Sea Inn
Chincoteague Area,
Virginia Eastern Shore
New Church, VA 23415
(804) 824-0672
Victoria Olian & Jack Betz
$75.00 to $105.00

Continental plus breakfast
In-house fine dining for dinner
5 rooms, 5 private baths
Children allowed
No pets
Restricted smoking
Mastercard, Visa, Am Ex, Discover

Elegant, European-style country inn, Mobil 3-star French-style restaurant. Luxurious rooms with antiques, Oriental rugs, Victorian detail, stained glass, bay windows. Afternoon tea. Beautiful beach and wildlife refuge nearby. Monthly chamber music - dinner concerts.

DESSERTS

BLUEBERRY APPLE CRISP

3 large tart apples, peeled & sliced
2 cups washed blueberries
1/2 cup sugar
Dash of salt
1 stick oleo, melted
1 cup quick cooking oatmeal
1/2 cup flour
1/2 cup brown sugar
1/2 cup chopped pecans

Layer apples, blueberries, sugar and salt, in that order, in an 8 1/2" x 11" baking dish. Mix remaining ingredients and sprinkle over top. Bake at 300° for 1 hour. Makes 8 servings.

Submitted by:

Seven Hills Inn
408 South Main St.
Lexington, VA 24450
(703) 463-4715
Jane Grigsby
$75.00 to $95.00

Continental plus breakfast
7 rooms, 5 private baths
Children allowed
No pets
Restricted smoking
Mastercard & Visa

Classic Southern manse in the heart of Lexington. Elegant accommodations furnished with family antiques and hand-crafted reproductions. Walk to fine restaurants, shops, Washington & Lee University, Virginia Military Institute and Visitor's Center. Suite available. Air-conditioned.

BLUEBERRY OR STRAWBERRY PIE

8 oz. cream cheese, softened
1 cup confectioner's sugar
1 cup Cool Whip topping
1 cup frozen blueberries or 1 cup sliced, frozen strawberries
1 - 9" unbaked pie crust
Chopped pecans

Blend cream cheese and confectioner's sugar with electric mixer until smooth. Fold in Cool Whip and fruit. Cover bottom of pie shell with chopped pecans, and bake at 375° until brown. Cool. Add cream cheese mixture and cover with remaining Cool Whip. Chill. Makes 1 - 9" pie.

Submitted by:

Sherwood Manor
Rt. 2, Box 267
Brodnax, VA 23920
(804) 848-0361
Grace B. Lucy
$75.00 to $95.00

Full breakfast
5 rooms, 5 private baths
Children, over 3
No pets
No smoking
Mastercard & Visa

Manor originally built as a church home for aged, infirm and disabled colored people, in the beautiful countryside of Brunswick County. Historical plantation, circa 1883, has been restored and furnished with period pieces for a glimpse of gentler times. Step back in history, relax and enjoy!

COLONIAL CHOCOLATE CAKE PÉCOUL

9 oz. chocolate chip morsels
3 tablespoons water
5 oz. melted butter

4 eggs, separated
1 1/2 cups sugar
3 tablespoons flour

Melt chocolate with 3 tablespoons water over low heat and stir until smooth. Add butter and egg yolks, stirring all the time. Add sugar. Beat egg whites until stiff, then stir them into the batter, and finally add the flour. Grease and flour a 9" diameter pan. Cook at 400° for 10 minutes and then 325° for 20 minutes. The cake is so gooey that it may not actually release from the pan, so you may have to leave it in the pan. Note: Pécoul is a 1769 plantation house in Martinique that used to be in our family.

Submitted by:

Newport House
710 South Henry Street
Williamsburg, VA 23185
(804) 229-1775
John & Cathy Millar
$90.00 to $120.00

Full breakfast
2 rooms, 2 private baths
Children allowed
No pets
No smoking

Reproduction of important 1756 house, totally furnished in period, including canopy beds. 5 minute walk from Historic Area, air conditioned, colonial recipes, colonial dancing every Tuesday evening. Host is author/historian, former museum director. Hostess is gardener, beekeeper, and 18th-century seamstress. Pet rabbit.

COCONUT MACAROONS

1 2/3 cups coconut
1/3 cup sugar
2 eggs

1 tablespoon butter, melted

Preheat oven to 350°. Grease 2 cookie sheets. Combine coconut and sugar. Beat eggs and melted butter well. Add to coconut mixture. Place 8 well-spaced mounds on each cookie sheet. Bake for 18 minutes, until golden. Watch carefully. Makes 16 cookies. Note: Upon discovering late one night that we were out of mints for the guests' pillows, my pantry search revealed a can of coconut. These cookies smelled wonderful while baking, and were such a hit, I now plan to use the macaroons for frequent guests.

Submitted by:

The Bedford House
422 Avenel Avenue
Bedford, VA 24523
(703) 586-5050
Lizbeth & Bob Laurrell
$50.00 to $65.00

2 rooms, 2 private baths
Children allowed
No pets
No smoking
Mastercard & Visa

Charming turn-of-the-century house filled with Southern hospitality, in a pretty little town, very close to the Blue Ridge Parkway.

COCONUT POUNDCAKE

1 1/2 cups Crisco
2 1/2 cups sugar
5 large eggs
1 cup sweet milk
1 teaspoon coconut flavoring

3 cups flour
1 teaspoon baking powder
1/4 teaspoon salt
1 1/4 cups coconut

Cream Crisco and sugar at high speed on mixer for 10 minutes. Add eggs one at a time. Sift dry ingredients and add to mixture, with milk and flavoring. Beat one minute. Fold in coconut. Grease and flour a tube pan (10" across top). Bake in oven that is not preheated, at 325° for 1 hour and 20 minutes. Remove from pan right away, and while hot place in box to keep moist. Freezes well. Can be frosted with a butter cream frosting or sprinkled with powdered sugar. Makes 25 servings.

Submitted by:

Maplewood Farm
Route 7, Box 461
Abingdon, VA 24210
(703) 628-2640
Doris Placak
$70.00

Full breakfast
3 rooms, 3 private baths
Children allowed
No pets
No smoking

Comfortable and beautiful 66 acre horse farm with woodland trails and lake. 6 miles from historic Abingdon, and Barter Theatre. Breakfast served in Garden Room or on outside deck overlooking the property. Handicapped facilities & overnight stabling for horses. Member of the Washington County Chamber of Commerce.

GRANDMA BESTPITCH'S HERMITS

1 cup butter
2 cups brown sugar
2 eggs
1/2 cup cold, strong coffee
1 cup raisins
1 cup black walnuts
1 rounded teaspoon nutmeg
1 teaspoon soda
1 teaspoon salt
3 1/2 cups flour

Cream butter and brown sugar. Add eggs. Mix in remainder of ingredients. Bake at 325° for 15 minutes. Makes 5 dozen cookies.

Submitted by:

The Mary Bladon House
381 Washington Ave., S.W.
Roanoke, VA 24016
(703) 344-5361
Bill & Sheri Bestpitch
$48.00 to $130.00

Full breakfast
3 rooms, 3 private baths
Children allowed
No pets
Restricted smoking
Mastercard & Visa

This lovely 1890's Victorian home offers accommodations reminiscent of a more gracious, slower-paced era - a time when elegant comfort was a way of life. Enjoy a charming step back in time for the young and the young at heart.

"JUST THE BEST POUND CAKE EVER!"

1 lb. real butter, softened, not melted
3 cups white sugar (or 2 cups white sugar and 1 cup brown sugar)
6 eggs
3 cups all-purpose flour
3/4 cup whole milk
1 teaspoon white vanilla
1 teaspoon almond or lemon extract
1/2 cup slivered almonds

Cream butter and sugar, then add eggs one at a time, beating well after each addition. Mix in flour and milk alternately. Then add vanilla and either almond or lemon extract. Treat tube pan with oil and flour, and pour in batter, sprinkling almonds around the top. Bake in 300° oven for one hour and forty minutes, until golden brown on top. Let cool for fifteen minutes, then turn out onto your fanciest cake platform. Guests love it at tea-time or for late dessert. Makes 18 slices.

Submitted by:

Abbie Hill Bed & Breakfast
P.O. Box 4503
Richmond, VA 23220
(804) 355-5855
Bill & Barbara Fleming
$55.00 to $95.00

Full breakfast
2 rooms, 2 private baths
Children, over 12
No pets
No smoking
Mastercard & Visa

In prestigous Monument Avenue Historic District, Federal brick 3-story townhouse is surrounded by many beautifully restored homes, apartment houses, and churches. Neighborhood restaurants for discriminating dinner tastes, in walking distance. Drive to museums, shopping, historic sites. Off-street parking.

LEGACY FRUIT SURPRISE

1 deep dish pie shell
1 pint whipping cream
1 can evaporated milk
1 can crushed pineapple
1 can cherry pie filling
2 sliced bananas
1/2 cup chopped walnuts

Bake pie shell. Whip whipping cream. Fold evaporated milk, pineapple, cherry pie filling, banana, and 1/4 cup walnuts into whipped cream. Then pour whipped cream mixture into pie shell. Sprinkle with the rest of the walnuts. Chill. Cut and serve.

Submitted by:

Legacy of Williamsburg Tavern
 & Bed & Breakfast Inn
930 Jamestown Road
Williamsburg, VA 23185
(800) 462-4722
(804) 220-0524
Mary Ann & Ed Lucas
$80.00 to $125.00

Full breakfast
4 rooms, 4 private baths
No children
No pets
No smoking
Mastercard & Visa

Careful thought was given to every detail of this early style American clapboard structure. Old-fashioned chimneys, various floor levels of radom pine flooring, and quaint rooms all speak of the colonial days. Bathrobes, tavern, game room, library, and keeping-billiards room. 18th century style at its finest.

MEANDER INN'S LEMON PUCKER CHEESECAKE

Crust:
2 pkgs. cellophane-wrapped Nabisco graham crackers
1/2 cup melted butter or margarine
1/2 cup sugar

Topping:
1 1/2 cups sour cream
1 teaspoon vanilla
1/2 cup powdered sugar

Filling:
3 lbs. cream cheese, softened
2 cups sugar
7 eggs
2 tablespoons cornstarch
Finely grated rind from 2 lemons
Juice from 2 lemons
1/4 cup cream

For crust: In food processor fitted with steel blade, crush graham crackers. Gradually mix in melted butter and sugar, scraping sides so butter is evenly mixed. Press mixture into 10" springform pan. Bake at 425° for 7 minutes. Remove from heat and let cool. For filling: Cream cheese and sugar in food processor until well-blended. Add eggs and beat well. Add remainder of ingredients and blend. Pour into cooled crust. Bake in 250° oven for 2 hours (if convection oven, bake 1 3/4 hours and test). Mix topping ingredients together. Remove pie and top with sour cream topping and bake 5 more minutes. Turn oven off and leave in oven with door slightly ajar to cool completely. Cover and chill at least 8 hours. Serves 16.

Submitted by:

The Meander Inn
Route 612
P.O. Box 443
Nellysford, VA 22958
(804) 361-1121
Kathy & Rick Cornelius
$60.00 to $80.00

Full breakfast
5 rooms, 5 private baths
Well-behaved and well-supervised children allowed
No pets
Restricted smoking
Mastercard & Visa

50 acre working farm, near Charlottesville & Wintergreen Resort, on the Rockfish River with panoramic view of Blue Ridge Mountains. Hiking, golf, skiing & fine dining nearby. Hot tub, open woodstove, country breakfast with farm fresh eggs. Owner-run and operated.

NORTH BEND'S PLANTATION PECAN PIE

1/4 cup margarine
1/2 cup sugar
1 cup light corn syrup
  (Karo)

3 eggs
1/4 teaspoon salt
1 cup pecans
1 uncooked pie shell

Cream together butter and sugar. Add Karo syrup and beat. Add eggs and beat. Add salt and pecans, and mix well. Pour into uncooked pie shell. Bake at 350° approximately 1 hour. Pie will be browned and won't shake in the middle. Yield: 1 delicious pie!!! Makes 6 - 8 servings.

Submitted by:

North Bend Plantation
12200 Weyanoke Road
Charles City, VA 23030
(804) 829-5176
George & Ridgely Copland
$95.00 to $118.00

Full breakfast
3 rooms, 3 private baths
Children, over 6
No pets
Restricted smoking

Greek Revival style plantation manor on National Register of Historic Places. Family-owned since 1819, 850 acres of land remain under cultivation. Rich Civil War history, beautiful spacious rooms, tester & canopy beds, swimming pool, croquet & lawn games. 30 minutes west of Colonial Williamsburg.

OZARK PUDDING

2 beaten eggs
1 cup dark brown sugar
1/2 cup sifted flour
2 teaspoons baking powder
1/2 teaspoon salt

2 teaspoons vanilla
1/2 cup chopped pecans or walnuts
1 cup chopped, peeled apple

Beat eggs and sugar until creamy. Stir in dry ingredients. Add vanilla, nuts and apple. Mix well. Pour into greased 9" deep dish pie pan. Bake 35 minutes at 350°. Serve warm with ice cream. Makes 6 - 8 servings.

Submitted by:

Homestay B&B
517 Richmond Road
Williamsburg, VA 23185
(804) 229-7468
Jim & Barbara Thomassen
$65.00 to $75.00

Full breakfast
2 rooms, 2 private baths
Children, over 5
No pets
No smoking
Mastercard & Visa

Cozy and convenient - 4 blocks to colonial Williamsburg and adjacent to College of William and Mary. Decorated with turn of the century family antiques and country charm. Homemade breads, and jellies made from herb garden plants.

PINEAPPLE PUDDING

6 slices white bread
1 can crushed pineapple
2 large eggs
1/3 cup sugar

2 tablespoons white corn syrup
1 teaspoon orange flavoring

Remove crust and cube bread. Place bread into greased casserole dish. Beat eggs into liquid of pineapple. Add pineapple pulp, and other remaining ingredients to egg mixture. Pour over cubed bread. Bake at 350° until inserted knife is removed clean.

Submitted by:

Evergreen Inn
P.O. Box 102
Pungoteague, VA 23422
(804) 442-3375
Catherine Johnson
$85.00 to $120.00

Full breakfast
2 rooms, 2 private baths
Children, over 12
No pets
Restricted smoking

18th century Georgian manor house on the Chesapeake Bay. 25 private acres with sandy beach, dock, paddle boat, crabbing, fishing and biking. Elegant guest rooms furnished with antiques and canopy beds. Gourmet breakfast.

QUICK & EASY PEANUT BUTTER PIE

3 oz. cream cheese
3/4 cup confectioner's sugar
1/3 cup milk
4 tablespoons crunchy peanut butter
6 oz. non-dairy whipped topping
1 - 9" pre-made chocolate cracker crumb crust
Chocolate fudge sauce
Fresh strawberries or maraschino cherries

Blend cream cheese and sugar with electric mixer until creamy. Add milk and peanut butter, mix thoroughly, and fold in whipped topping. Pour into pre-made crust and freeze 2 hours or until firm. To serve, cut while frozen, pour about a tablespoon of heated fudge sauce over each slice, and garnish with strawberry or cherry. Can be served frozen or left about 30 minutes to thaw. Makes 8 servings.

Submitted by:

Milton Hall Bed & Breakfast Inn
RR# 3
Covington, VA 24426
(703) 965-0196
John & Vera Eckert
$75.00 to $140.00

Full breakfast
6 rooms, 6 private baths
Children allowed
Pets allowed
Smoking allowed
Mastercard & Visa

English country manor house, circa 1874, with spacious rooms, antiques, period reproductions and unique collectibles, fireplaces, and queen size beds. Hiking, bicycling, fishing, hunting, mineral baths, covered bridges, and the many attractions at The Homestead.

"THE SPRINGS" APRICOT CAKE

1 lb. pitted dates
1 lb. dried apricots
6 ozs. pitted prunes (halved)
1/2 cup raisins
1/2 lb. shelled walnuts
1/2 lb. shelled pecans

1 1/2 cups unbleached flour
1 teaspoon baking powder
1 teaspoon salt
6 eggs
1 cup sugar
2 teaspoons vanilla

Line a 6 cup round cake tube pan with brown paper. Combine fruit and nuts in large bowl. Sift flour and baking powder over fruit and nuts. Mix until well-coated. Beat salt, eggs, sugar and vanilla until foamy. Pour egg mixture over fruit and nuts. Combine thoroughly and gently. Fill pan, press in mixture. Stud cake with additional nuts. Bake at 300° for 1 1/4 hours. Makes 16 servings.

Submitted by:

Shenandoah Springs
HC 6, Box 122
Madison, VA 22727
(703) 923-4300
Anne & Douglas Farmer
$65.00 to $120.00

Full breakfast
6 rooms, 3 1/2 private baths
Children allowed
No pets
Restricted smoking

Relax on 1,000 acres of forest land, meadows, shady lanes, bridle trails and scenic views. Fishing, canoeing, ice skating on Shenandoah Springs Lake, and cross-country skiing on our trails. Fireplaces, cozy bedrooms, cabins available. Wilderness hideaway!

UPSIDE DOWN CHOCOLATE PUDDING

2 squares unsweetened chocolate
2 tablespoons butter
1 cup flour
3/4 cup sugar

Topping:
1/2 cup white sugar
1/2 cup brown sugar
2 tablespoons cocoa

2 teaspoons baking powder
1/4 teaspoon salt
1/2 cup chopped walnuts
1/2 cup milk
1 teaspoon vanilla

1 cup cold water or cold coffee

Melt chocolate and butter together, set aside. Sift next four ingredients together into large mixing bowl. Add walnuts, milk, vanilla and the melted butter and chocolate. Mix well and place in buttered, round casserole dish. Sift topping ingredients together over top of batter. Pour water (or coffee) over this. Do not mix. Baked batter will come to the top, with sauce in bottom of dish. Bake at 350° for 30 minutes. Serve warm with ice cream. Makes 8 servings.

Submitted by:

Fairview Bed & Breakfast
Route 4, Box 117
Amherst, VA 24521
(804) 277-8500
Judy & Jim Noon
$40.00 to $65.00

Full breakfast
3 rooms, 1 private bath
Children allowed
Well-behaved pets allowed with prior reservation
Smoking allowed
Mastercard & Visa

Brick Italianate farmhouse surrounded by pastures & rolling fields with beautiful Blue Ridge Mountain views. Informal lifestyle with feeling of the Victorian Age. Spacious guest rooms furnished with antiques. In Amherst County, near the Parkway, where fabulous sunsets, fine food and fresh air await.

Visiting Virginia

Virginia is a commonwealth of uncommon beauty and richly elaborate history, a history that is America's history. The first permanent English settlement was established in Jamestown in 1607. The roots of the American Revolution were put down in Virginia. Williamsburg became the new nation's first capital. More than 60 percent of the Civil War battles were fought on Virginia soil. The commonwealth is also known as the Mother of Presidents, home to eight of the nation's chief executives, including George Washington, Thomas Jefferson, James Madison, and James Monroe.

There are few states more strikingly beautiful than Virginia. Mountains, seashores, gardens, rivers, and woodlands abound! The true appeal of Virginia is its variety. Beautiful beaches, exciting cities, thrilling theme parks, magnificent mountains, outstanding outdoor recreation, and more history than any other U.S. state, Virginia is for lovers of all that and more.

Six distinct geographic regions offer the traveller infinite possibilities for exploration and experience:

THE NORTHERN REGION extends from Washington, D.C. south through the rolling countryside to Orange. The area offers historic sites like Mount Vernon, Montpelier, and Civil War battlegrounds, as well as sophisticated shops and gourmet dining.

THE CENTRAL REGION'S rolling foothills on the eastern slope of the Blue Ridge Mountains offer a great variety of interesting sights and activities - wineries, antique shops, national forests, recreational lakes, and historic areas such as Thomas Jefferson's Monticello and Appomattox. Regional festivals are special events in Charlottesville, Richmond, Lynchburg, and Danville, the hub cities.

THE SHENANDOAH REGION boasts orchards, caverns, Civil War sites, and the spectacular Blue Ridge Mountains. The Skyline Drive and The Blue Ridge Parkway run the length of the Shenandoah Valley from Front Royal, through Staunton, Lexington, and Roanoke.

THE SOUTHWESTERN REGION has been called the "Grand Canyon of the South". Its acres of untouched forest, powerful waterfalls and quiet lakes and streams offer a welcome respite from civilization. Abingdon is the home of the famous Barter Theatre.

THE TIDEWATER REGION is the land of patriots, plantations, and pristine beaches. Williamsburg, Norfolk, and Virginia Beach offer the traveller history, culture, and miles of beaches for recreation.

THE EASTERN SHORE REGION is the home of quiet fishing villages, the beautiful Chesapeake Bay, and the wild ponies of Chincoteague. Miles of unspoiled beaches provide an ideal getaway.

The discerning traveller exploring Virginia may add another dimension to the unique experience of each region by staying at Bed and Breakfasts. These accommodations are highly individualized, each reflecting the tastes and lifestyles of the innkeeper as well as the atmosphere of the region.

For more information about travel in Virginia, contact The Virginia Division of Tourism at 1-800-VISIT-VA.

A comprehensive directory of B&B lodgings throughout Virginia is available by writing: The Bed and Breakfast Association of Virginia, P.O. Box 791, Orange, Virginia 22960.

VIRGINIA MAP
(Western Half)

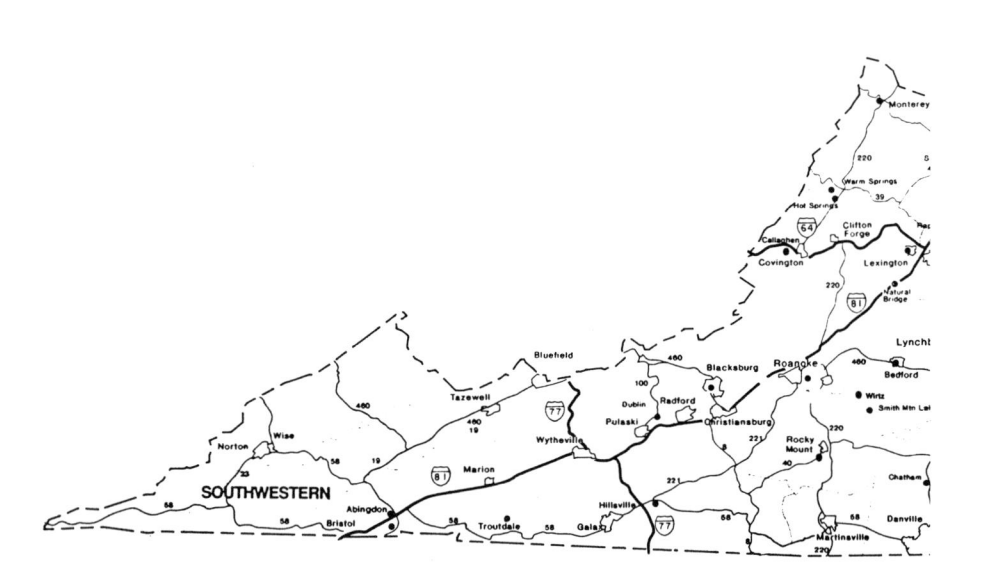

VIRGINIA MAP
(Eastern Half)

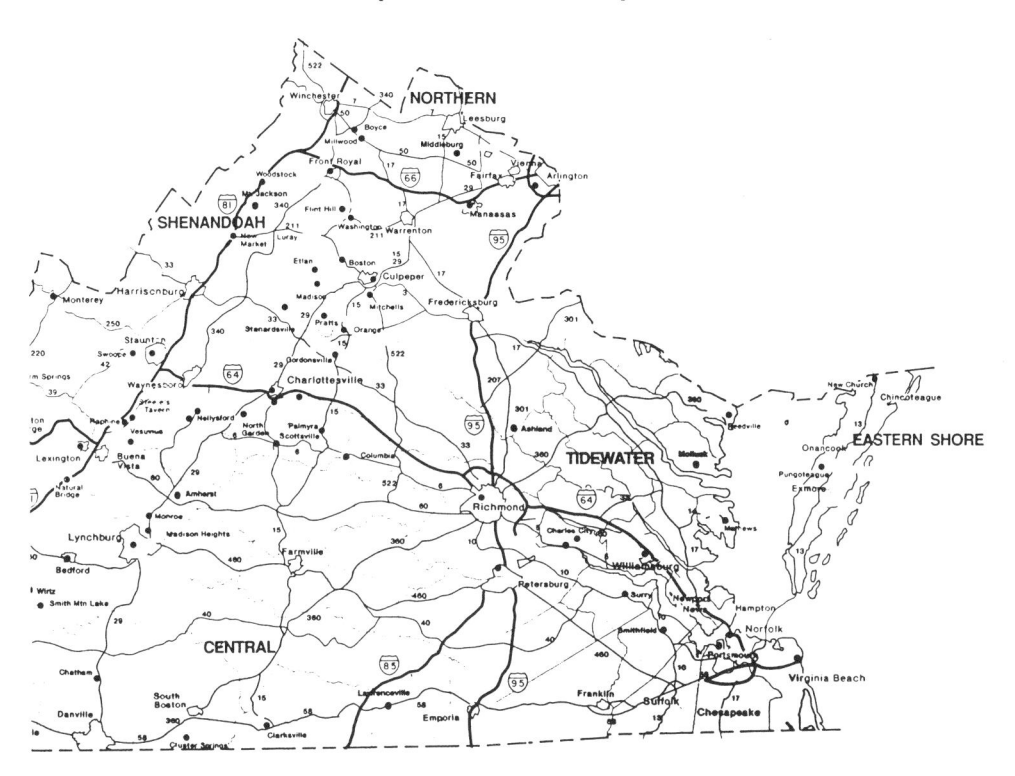

INDEX OF BED & BREAKFASTS

ABINGDON
　Cabin on the River 56
　Maplewood Farm 93
　Victoria & Albert Inn
　　& Antiques........................83
AMHERST
　Dulwich Manor....................44
　Fairview B&B....................103
ARLINGTON
　Memory House...................76
ASHLAND
　The Henry Clay Inn.............29
BEDFORD
　The Bedford House............92
BLACKSBURG
　L'Arche Farm B&B..............12
BOSTON
　Thistle Hill B&B...................31
BRODNAX
　Sherwood Manor................90
CHARLES CITY
　North Bend Plantation........98
CLARKSVILLE
　Needmore Inn 16
CHARLOTTESVILLE
　The Inn at Monticello..........20
　Old Slave Quarters.............55
CHATHAM
　House of Laird....................66
　Sims-Mitchell House B&B...37
CLIFTON FORGE
　Firmstone Manor B&B Inn...45
CLUSTER SPRINGS
　Oak Grove Plantation 34
COLUMBIA
　Upper Byrd Farm B&B........81
COVINGTON
　Milton Hall B&B Inn...........101
FLINT HILL
　Caledonia Farm B&B..........39
FRONT ROYAL
　Chester House...................77

GORDONSVILLE
　Norfields Farm B&B............61
　Sleepy Hollow Farm B&B....63
HILLSVILLE
　Bray's Manor......................13
HOT SPRINGS
　King's Victorian Inn 71
LEESBURG
　Fleetwood Farm B&B.........18
LEXINGTON
　Fassifern B&B 57
　Lavender Hill Farm 40
　Llewellyn Lodge..................42
　Seven Hills Inn....................89
LYNCHBURG
　Langhorne Manor...............70
　Lynchburg Mansion Inn
　　Bed & Breakfast................73
　The Madison House
　　Bed & Breakfast................86
MADISON
　Shenandoah Springs.......102
MADISON HEIGHTS
　Winridge Bed & Breakfast...49
MATHEWS
　Ravenswood Inn................24
MOLLUSK
　Greenvale Manor................36
MONROE
　"St. Moor" House...............84
MOUNT JACKSON
　The Widow Kip's.................68
NATURAL BRIDGE
　Burger's Country Inn..........72
NELLYSFORD
　The Meander Inn 97
　Trillium House......................7
　Upland Manor....................82
NEW CHURCH
　The Garden and
　　the Sea Inn.......................87

NEW MARKET
Red Shutter Farmhouse.......8
NORFOLK
Page House Inn..................52
NORTH GARDEN
The Inn at the Crossroads...41
ORANGE
The Holladay House...........60
PALMYRA
Danscot House..................27
PUNGOTEAGUE
Evergreen Inn 100
RAPHINE
Oak Spring Farm &
Vineyard 64
REEDVILLE
Cedar Grove......................10
RICHMOND
Abbie Hill B&B...................95
Mr. Patrick Henry's Inn........85
The William Catlin House 80
West-Bocock House 11
ROANOKE
The Mary Bladon House.....94
ROCKY MOUNT
The Claiborne House.........58
SCOTTSVILLE
High Meadows
Vineyard Inn......................38
SMITHFIELD
Isle of Wight Inn 53
SMITH MOUNTAIN LAKE
The Manor at
Taylor's Store 17
STANARDSVILLE
Edgewood Farm B&B 74
STAUNTON
Ashton Country House 65
Frederick House................33
The Sampson Eagon Inn....30
Thornrose House 21

STEELE'S TAVERN
The Osceola Mill
Country Inn 43
SURRY
Seward House Inn 79
SWOOPE
Lambsgate B&B.................19
VIRGINIA BEACH
Barclay Cottage 50
WARM SPRINGS
Anderson Cottage B&B.....46
WASHINGTON
Heritage House, Inc. 62
Sycamore Hill
House & Gardens 47
WAYNESBORO
The Iris Inn........................26
WILLIAMSBURG
Applewood Colonial B&B...54
Colonial Capital B&B 35
Erika's Cottage 51
Governor's Trace B&B........78
Hite's B&B 14
Homestay B&B..................99
Legacy of Williamsburg
Tavern and B&B Inn...........96
Liberty Rose B&B...............23
Newport House 91
Piney Grove at
Southall's Plantation 28
Williamsburg Sampler
Bed & Breakfast................75
WOODSTOCK
Azalea House B&B............22
The Country Fare B&B.........9
The Inn at
Narrow Passage................69

NOTES

NOTES

ORDER FORMS

OVERNIGHT SENSATIONS: Recipes From Virginia's Finest Bed & Breakfasts

I would like to order *OVERNIGHT SENSATIONS: Recipes From Virginia's Finest Bed & Breakfasts*. I have indicated the quantity below. <u>MAIL THIS ORDER TO</u>: Winters Publishing, P.O. Box 501, Greensburg, IN 47240.

_____ OVERNIGHT SENSATIONS $9.95 each _____

Shipping Charge $2.00 each _____

Sales Tax (Indiana residents <u>ONLY</u>) $ .60 each _____

TOTAL _____

Please send to:

Name: _____

Address: _____

City: _____ State: _____ Zip: _____

OVERNIGHT SENSATIONS: Recipes From Virginia's Finest Bed & Breakfasts

I would like to order *OVERNIGHT SENSATIONS: Recipes From Virginia's Finest Bed & Breakfasts*. I have indicated the quantity below. <u>MAIL THIS ORDER TO</u>: Winters Publishing, P.O. Box 501, Greensburg, IN 47240.

_____ OVERNIGHT SENSATIONS $9.95 each _____

Shipping Charge $2.00 each _____

Sales Tax (Indiana residents <u>ONLY</u>) $ .60 each _____

TOTAL _____

Please send to:

Name: _____

Address: _____

City: _____ State: _____ Zip: _____
